Certificate of Baptism

Date of Birth _____

I certify that, in obedience to our Lord
Jesus Christ, and in imitation of His example,
_____, *was, this day,*

buried with Him in Baptism.

_____
Witness

_____
Place

GOING ON TO MATURITY

Steps in Spiritual Growth

by
Rubel Shelly

20th Century Christian
2809 Granny White Pike
Nashville, TN 37204

Table of Contents

Dedication

This book is dedicated to
the faithful members of the

Estes Church of Christ
Henderson, Tennessee

and the

Ashwood Church of Christ
Nashville, Tennessee

who gave such a gracious reception
to this material as it neared its final form.

Preface

Of his ministry on behalf of Christ, Paul wrote: "Him we proclaim, warning every man and teaching every man in all wisdom, that we may present *every man mature in Christ.* For this I toil, striving with all the energy which he mightily inspires within me" (Col. 1:28-29 RSV).

Every man mature in Christ! Imagine what it would mean to the fortunes of the church of Christ if this goal were to be achieved. The world would not be able to withstand the charge we could mount against the strongholds of Satan! And even if we do not achieve the goal of *every* man and woman mature in Christ, we must encourage and help each child of God who is willing to nurture spiritual growth in his or her daily life.

Over the years of my own attempts to grow into the likeness of Jesus Christ, I have sought materials to read which would contribute to those efforts. It became apparent that this is an area which has been neglected among us. We have produced many volumes on first principles which are designed to lead men and women to the Lord; we have produced very few volumes which offer specific and practical suggestions about how to go on to maturity. Thus I have tried to gather materials of this sort and have taught many classes and preached many sermons on the theme of Christian growth.

I do not consider my own spiritual growth to be complete. Far from it, I know my weaknesses and inadequacies only too well. But the material contained in this book has been useful to me, and others who have studied it with me in various settings have claimed to profit from it as well. It is hoped that many more of God's people will find it of value as they study the material in printed form.

I must thank my wife, Myra, and my secretary, Cheryl Fewell, for typing the final manuscript of this book. My thanks also to Neil Bryan for encouraging me to write this book. Above all, I thank a gracious God for the ministry of writing which he has entrusted to me and a kind brotherhood which has been willing to use the several volumes I have produced.

That God shall be glorified and his people encouraged to spiritual growth by means of this book is its author's prayer.

Rubel Shelly

GOING ON TO MATURITY

Chapter One

WHAT HAS HAPPENED TO ME?

Conversion is the turning of one's whole being, in both heart and life, from the love and practice of sin to the love and service of God. This process is described in different ways in Scripture. Each description uses imagery which is designed to impress us with the implications of what it means to be saved. Each is beautiful and powerful in its own right.

As you read the following passages, pay particular attention to the words and phrases which are in italics and reflect on their significance. "Repent ye therefore, and turn again, that *your sins may be blotted out,* that so there may come seasons of refreshing from the presence of the Lord ... " (Acts 3:19). The Lord told Saul of Tarsus that he had been appointed as a special minister to the Gentiles "*to open their eyes,* that they may *turn from darkness to light and from the power of Satan unto God,* that they may receive *remission of sins* and an *inheritance among them that are sanctified by faith* in me" (Acts 26:18). "And you did he *make alive,* when ye were dead through your trespasses and sins" (Eph. 2:1).

Many more verses could be added to this list, but these are sufficient for demonstrating that conversion is presented in the Word of God as a radical occurrence of great spiritual importance.

Please take note of the fact that these verses describe conversion as an objective fact accomplished by the power of God. They do not describe it in terms of subjective experiences which cannot bear public investigation and verification.

Sometimes an individual's conversion is sudden and dramatic; at other times it is the completion of a prolonged and gradual process of deliberate approach unto God. Saul of Tarsus was on his way to persecute Christians at Damascus when the Lord appeared to him and set the stage for his conversion. When Ananias came to him with the commands of the gospel for his salvation, this man who had been a violent enemy of Christ only a few hours before was eager to become his disciple and messenger (cf. Acts 9, 22, 26). On the other hand, a Roman centurion named Cornelius had been consciously seeking to learn the will of God so that he could submit to it. Far from fighting Christ and persecuting Christians, he had been learning of the true God (evidently from the Jews of his city) and praying to know the will of this God for his life. When Peter was dispatched to Cornelius' house in answer to those prayers, his conversion was the final step in a long and conscious process of drawing near to the Lord (cf. Acts 10-11).

2

The paths of Saul and Cornelius to the blessed state of salvation had been very different. Though they believed and obeyed the same gospel, the circumstances of their learning it and the manner of their being made ready to receive it were quite unlike. So it is with individuals today. No one should feel that his or her conversion is less real or effective because it was not so dramatic as that of Saul or someone else. The test of true conversion is not drama or immediacy; it is correspondence with the truth and a changed life which bears the fruit of the Spirit of God.

When an individual has been saved, there is always to be this realization: "Wherefore if any man is in Christ, he is a new creature: the old things are passed away; behold, they are become new" (2 Cor. 5:17). How well I remember the scene of the immersion of a friend of mine. When I raised him from the water, he smiled broadly and said, "I feel like a new man!" On the basis of this statement from Paul, I was able to respond, "You *are* a new man."

It is an important step in one's spiritual growth to appreciate the significance of what happens to him in the process of salvation. So this is where we begin our series of lessons on the theme of growth and maturity in Christ.

In this study, we shall attempt to gain a more complete understanding of the meaning of salvation. *By virtue of my conversion, what has happened to me?*

The Saved Person is "In Christ"

The words "in Christ," "in Jesus Christ," or their equivalent are reported by one commentator to appear 55 times in the New Testament, and 54 of these instances are in the writings of Paul. If a straw in the wind shows which way it is blowing, statistics of this sort surely reveal a

3

channel of thought in the apostle's mind which we would do well to investigate. What is the significance of being "in Christ"?

For one thing, such a person has been released from the guilt and power of sin. "There is therefore now no condemnation to them that are *in Christ Jesus*" (Rom. 8:1). For another, he has been given a right relationship (i.e., righteousness) with deity. "What is more, I consider everything a loss compared to the surpassing greatness of knowing Christ Jesus my Lord, for whose sake I have lost all things. I consider them rubbish, that I may gain Christ and be found *in him,* not having a righteousness of my own that comes from the law, but that which is through faith *in Christ* – the righteousness that comes from God and is by faith" (Phil. 3:8-9 NIV). Again, "Him who knew no sin he made to be sin on our behalf; that we might become the righteousness of God *in him*" (2 Cor. 5:21). Other things said to be "in Christ" are spiritual blessings (Eph. 1:3), redemption (Eph. 1:7), salvation (2 Tim. 2:10), and many more.

One attains the status of being "in Christ" at the time of his immersion for the remission of sins. "For as many of you as were *baptized into Christ* did put on Christ" (Gal. 3:27). "Or are ye ignorant that all we who were *baptized into Christ Jesus* were baptized into his death? We were buried therefore with him through baptism into death: that like as Christ was raised from the dead through the glory of the Father, so we also might walk in newness of life" (Rom. 6:3-4).

As Paul expressed it in a verse noted earlier (2 Cor. 5:17), the person who has been baptized into Christ has all things "become new" for him. He has a *new name* to

4

wear; he is a Christian (Acts 11:26). He has *new relation-ships* in his spiritual life; he is a child of God and a brother to every other Christian in the world (Gal. 3:26-28). He has a *new standard* for his conduct; he lives for the purpose of glorifying God in his deeds (Eph. 2:1-10). He has *new objects of affection;* he no longer loves the world but has his heart fixed on the heavenly things of the Lord (Col. 3:1-3). He has *new interests* to employ his energies; he puts the kingdom of God first in all his decisions and deeds (Matt. 6:33).

The saved person not only is "in Christ," he also has *Christ in him.* Paul exclaimed, "I have been crucified with Christ; and it is no longer I that live, but Christ liveth in me" (Gal. 2:20a; cf. Rom. 8:10; Eph. 3:17; Col. 1:27). This relationship is no "mystical union" of Paul's imagination. It is a real relationship between the believer and his Lord. It is made possible through the indwelling Spirit of Christ in the believer and shows itself in ever-increasing devotion and righteousness in a Christian's life (cf. Chapter Three).

What beautiful twin truths! The saved person is in Christ, and Christ is in the saved person. The new convert has been incorporated into the spiritual body of Christ, the church; the Spirit of Christ has taken up his abode in the new convert. By virtue of the former fact, the Christian knows that the past is forgiven and taken care of by the blood of Christ; by virtue of the latter one, he can be confident of his ability to live the new life of righteousness by the power of God.

Jesus' Figure of Conversion: "Born Anew"

Turning now to the language of Jesus himself, there

could be no more beautiful picture of salvation than the one he painted with words to Nicodemus. He told this Jewish official that conversion was like starting life all over again. He called it a *new birth*. "Jesus answered and said unto him, Verily, verily, I say unto thee, Except one be born anew, he cannot see the kingdom of God. Nicodemus saith unto him, How can a man be born when he is old? Can he enter a second time into his mother's womb, and be born? Jesus answered, Verily, verily, I say unto thee, Except one be born of water and the Spirit, he cannot enter into the Kingdom of God. That which is born of the flesh is flesh; and that which is born of the Spirit is spirit. Marvel not that I said unto thee, Ye must be born anew" (John 3:3-7).

Physical birth cannot bring spiritual life. There must be a spiritual birth for one to enter and share in the blessings of the kingdom of God. According to Jesus, this birth is "of water and the Spirit." It is a single event involving two related elements. The external rite associated with the new birth is baptism (i.e., immersion in water); the actual power which brings about the spiritual rebirth of an individual is from above (i.e., the Holy Spirit). The effectiveness of baptism is not in its administrator or in the water itself (cf. 1 Cor. 1:17; 1 Pet. 3:21) but in the divine power which works in connection with our obedience to God in submitting to immersion in Jesus' name.

The Holy Spirit begets men unto new life through the seed of the kingdom, the Word of God. Men are "begotten again, not of corruptible seed, but of incorruptible, through the word of God, which liveth and abideth" (1 Pet. 1:23). As the Spirit of God leads an individual to faith, repentance, and confession of Christ through the saving gospel,

6

that person obeys Christ in baptism. At that point, he is cleansed and quickened, and the Spirit of God takes up residence in him. "Peter replied, 'Repent and be baptized, every one of you, in the name of Jesus Christ so that your sins may be forgiven. And you will receive the gift of the Holy Spirit'" (Acts 2:38 NIV). As J. W. McGarvey pointed out in his excellent commentary on Acts, the expression "gift of the Holy Spirit" in this familiar verse has reference "to that indwelling of the Holy Spirit by which we bring forth the fruits of the Spirit, and without which we are not of Christ." When this process of obedience to the gospel has been completed in the life of any individual, he or she has been born anew!

A related passage which constitutes a good apostolic commentary on Jesus' statement about the new birth is found in Paul's letter to the Ephesians. Speaking of the body of Christ as a whole rather than of specific individuals, he wrote of how "Christ also loved the church, and gave himself up for it; that he might sanctify it, having cleansed it by the washing of water with the word" (Eph. 5:26). This verse stresses again that the act of baptism (i.e., "washing of water") has its real power by virtue of its connection with "the word" (i.e., God's promise associated with the act of immersion).

Paul takes up the same idea of rebirth (Gr, *palingenesia* = again + birth) in Titus 3:5. "Not by works done in righteousness, which we did ourselves, but according to his mercy he saved us, through the washing of regeneration and renewing of the Holy Spirit." He again associates spiritual rebirth with baptism (i.e., "washing of regeneration") and the Spirit of God (i.e., "renewing of the Holy Spirit"). "The washing and the reception of the Spirit are

7

here seen as a unity. Regeneration comes about through water and the Spirit (cf. Jn. 3:5)." (*New International Dictionary of New Testament Theology* I: 185.)

Can you imagine a more beautiful way to present the concept of salvation to men? No language could have been chosen which would make it more desirable. Poets have longed for "the land of beginning again," and all men and women with sensitive spirits have wished they could "start all over again" with their lives. It is not just a dream! It is a real possibility because of Jesus Christ!

People can begin anew before the Almighty. They can experience salvation and renewal by means of the birth of water and Spirit which Jesus discussed. Life *can* begin again.

Some New Testament Words and Expressions

There are so many expressive images by means of which the Bible presents the conversion concept to us that space does not permit a close examination of each. Here are a few of the more prominent ones which should be reflected on at least briefly in the course of this study.

Redemption. This word originally referred to the buying back of a slave or captive, making him free by the payment of a ransom. It is used figuratively in the New Testament of a person's release from the guilt and bondage of sin. Christians have been "justified freely by his grace through the redemption that is in Christ Jesus" (Rom. 3:24). It is in Christ that "we have our redemption, the forgiveness of our sins" (Col. 1:14).

The Bible speaks of us as "slaves of sin" (John 8:34) and as being "sold under sin" (Rom. 7:14). Jesus has liberated us by buying us for himself with the purchase price of his own blood. "Knowing that ye were redeemed, not with corruptible things, with silver or gold, from your vain manner of life handed down from your fathers; but with precious blood, as of a lamb without blemish and without spot, even the blood of Christ" (1 Pet. 1:18-19).

A little boy lost his prize sailboat in a swift stream. It had cost him several weeks of allowance, and he was broken-hearted over the loss. A few days after the incident, he saw his sailboat in the possession of another child who had found it downstream. He negotiated with the boy, saved his money again, and bought the boat from him. When he took it from him, he clutched it to himself and said, "Little sailboat, now you are twice mine!" Saved people are twice God's. We were his by right of creation – but drifted away from him because of our sin. He gave the precious blood of Jesus to buy us back, to redeem us, to make us his a second time.

Calling and Election. A different expression is used by Peter to dramatize the nature of salvation when he writes: "Wherefore, brethren, give the more diligence to make your calling and election sure" (2 Pet. 1:10a).

Heaven calls and elects people unto salvation, but it is never done in a coercive manner. God *calls* all people unto himself through the preaching of the gospel. Paul expressed it this way: "He called you through our gospel, to the obtaining of the glory of our Lord Jesus Christ" (2 Thess. 2:14). This call goes out to men of every race, tongue, and nation of the world. Then he *elects* unto salvation those who put themselves into the sphere of his grace through obedience to that gospel. In my home state, "straight ticket voting" was once allowed. One could walk into a voting booth and pull one lever to vote for

9

every Republican on the ballot or for every Democrat on it. By way of analogy, it is as if all people have their names on one of two "tickets," i.e., Obedience or Disobedience, Faith or Unbelief. God is voting a straight ticket! He elects all the Obedience Party unto eternal life; he votes the Faith ticket in support of all those who have received the Son.

This expression emphasizes that the initiative in salvation was taken by heaven. Deity saw us heading for damnation, called us back, and elected those who would respond to that call unto salvation. And, as Jesus put it, no man could have come to him as Savior "except it be given unto him of the Father" (John 6:65). But this gracious calling of the Lord can be resisted, voided, or received in vain (cf. 2 Cor. 6:1). Our calling and election are "made sure" only by our obedient faith. "Wherefore, brethren, give the more diligence to make your calling and election sure: for *if ye do these things,* ye shall never stumble" (2 Pet. 1:10).

Justification. This term comes from a family of words related to right conduct, uprightness, following the will of God so as to be free of blame at the Judgment. Since all men have sinned (Rom. 3:23), all men are under condemnation (Rom. 6:23). Therefore justification is a state which men are unable to attain on our own. As Paul uses the term in Romans, it refers to that divine action by means of which God releases men from the sentence of death.

This work of justification has been realized through the vicarious death of Jesus Christ. "Being justified freely by his grace through the redemption that is in Christ Jesus: whom God set forth to be a propitiation, through faith, in his blood, to show his righteousness because of the passing over of the sins done aforetime, in the forbearance of God; for the showing, I say, of his righteousness at this present season: that he might himself be just, and the justifier of him that hath faith in Jesus" (Rom. 3:24-26). According to this text, divine justice was served in that the penalty due for sin was exacted; Jesus absorbed the judgment incurred by human sin. By means of the atoning blood shed in that act, heaven is able to offer release from condemnation to all those who believe in Jesus. As Paul later expressed it: "Much more then, being now justified by his blood, shall we be saved from the wrath of God through him" (Rom. 5:9).

All this means that the Christian stands before God free of the sentence of death. But this is so not because of his own goodness; it is due to the action of God on his behalf.

Reconciliation. "But all things are of God, who reconciled us to himself through Christ, and gave unto us the ministry of reconciliation; to wit, that God was in Christ reconciling the world unto himself, not reckoning unto them their trespasses, and having committed unto us the word of reconciliation. We are ambassadors therefore on behalf of Christ, as though God were entreating by us: we beseech you on behalf of Christ, be ye reconciled to God" (2 Cor. 5:18-20).

Reconciliation has to do with the overcoming of barriers between persons. In the case of man and God, the barrier between them is sin. Mankind's sinfulness has separated us from God and made a right relationship with deity impossible (cf. Isa. 59:1-2). With man unable to surmount or destroy that barrier, God acted on our behalf through Christ. The blood of the Son of God has accomplished

11

what nothing else could. By means of the cross, a path of free access into divine grace has been opened to the human race.

At the same time, all those who have been put at peace with God through this wonderful reconciliation are also at peace with one another. The death of Jesus not only reconciled man to his God but also reconciled man to his fellow men. "For he is our peace, who made both one, and brake down the middle wall of partition ... that he might create in himself of the two one new man, so making peace; and might reconcile them both in one body unto God through the cross, having slain the enmity thereby" (Eph. 2:14-16). Jew and Gentile, male and female, black and white, rich and poor, educated and illiterate – not one of these distinctions is of consequence in the body of Christ. We are one with God and one with each other. We have been reconciled.

Forgiveness. This is probably the term we think of and use most often when we think about the meaning of salvation. To be saved is to be forgiven.

To forgive is to release, to send away, to pardon. As the word applies to sin, it is to let it go and treat the person who committed the sin as if it had never occurred at all. It is not to be confused with *indulgence,* for it requires that certain conditions be satisfied before it can be realized. Neither is it to be regarded as *something earned,* for it is the free gift of God to men and women.

The most wonderful fact in all the Bible is that *God forgives sin.* He does not ignore it, and he cannot approve it. Because of his grace, however, he can and does forgive it. When we come to Jesus Christ in trusting, obedient faith, he releases us from the guilt of our sins and treats us as if they had never been committed.

You Are a Saint

The final point to be made in this chapter is the following: *You are a saint!* Don't let this assertion startle you, for it is true. If you have been saved from sin by grace through faith, heaven regards you as a saint and expects you to live as one. Just what does this imply?

Our English word "saint" conveys the notion of one who is sinless and above the rest of mortals. As it is used in the New Testament, however, it translates a Greek word (*hagios*) which has quite a different meaning. A person or thing is *hagios* when it is devoted to the possession and service of God. For example, the temple at Jerusalem was *hagios,* for is was dedicated to exclusive use as a place of worship to the Lord; a sacrifice being prepared for the temple altar was *hagios,* for it was to be offered to the Almighty and could not be used for any other purpose. In the same way, a Christian is *hagios;* he is set apart as one who belongs exclusively to the possession and service of God (cf. Rom. 8:27; 12:13; Eph. 2:19; Phil. 4:22).

So when the Bible refers to Christians as "saints," it does not imply that they are sinless and perfect. It means that Christians are different from other people because they belong to God and to his service.

By virtue of your conversion to Christ, you have pledged yourself to God. You must live every moment of your life in the awareness that you are his. You must make your decisions and order your life as one who puts spiritual considerations above all other things.

Conclusion

Yes, marvelous things have happened to you by the grace and power of God because of your conversion to Christ. You need to reflect on these things with much study and prayer, for it is an important step in one's spiritual growth to realize exactly what has happened already in being saved from sin.

Yet even more wonderful evidences of God's transforming power are ahead for you in the life you are called to live in Christ. "Now unto him that is able to do exceeding abundantly above all that we ask or think, according to the power that worketh in us, unto him be the glory in the church and in Christ Jesus unto all generations for ever and ever. Amen" (Eph. 3:20-21).

In lessons to come, we will be examining the ways and means of God to accomplish these things in our lives. If such a study is undertaken with full seriousness of purpose, it will enrich our understanding and open up possibilities for our spiritual development. It will aid us in *going on to maturity.*

Some Things To Think About

1. Give your own definition of *conversion*. Is the experience subjective or objective in character? What is the proper test of one's conversion experience?

2. Discuss the significance of being "in Christ." From your own research, compile a complete list of the things said to be "in Christ."

3. What are some of the popular notions of what the new birth is? How do these differ from what the New Testament teaches?

4. Several New Testament references to conversion are listed in one section of this chapter (e.g., redemption, calling and election, etc.). Expand the brief comments made about each of these by adding your own thoughts and locating more texts related to each. Which do you find most meaningful?

5. The concept of "sainthood" is a confused one among religious people of our time. Could you explain and clarify it to someone who doesn't understand it?

6. Why is a study of the significance of conversion an important first step in our effort to understand the means to spiritual growth and maturity? What helpful insights have you gained from this study?

7. In anticipation of later studies from this book, conduct a class discussion on the following question: What do you believe to be the most important ingredient in a truly spiritual life?

Chapter Two

NOW WHAT?

I am a Christian. By virtue of my faith in Christ which moved me to repent of my sins and be baptized, I am "in Christ" and have been "born of water and the Spirit." The past has been forgiven by the blood of Christ, and I am in right relationship with God. But what do I do now? Where do I go from here?

The unnamed writer of the book of Hebrews helps us get this issue in perspective. As he writes to Christians of his day about their need of growth and development in spiritual things, he forces us to think of our own situation. In the sixth chapter of the book, look closely at what he says.

First, he states the *divine expectation* of believers: *Christians are expected to make progress in their spiritual lives.* "Therefore let us leave the elementary teachings about Christ and go on to maturity, not laying again the foundation of repentance from acts that lead to death, and of faith in God, instruction about baptisms, the laying on of hands, the resurrection of the dead, and eternal judgment. And God permitting, we will do this" (Heb. 6:1-3 NIV).

Second, he sounds a *warning* to his readers: *failure to grow brings condemnation.* "It is impossible for those who have once been enlightened, who have tasted the heavenly gift, who have shared in the Holy Spirit, who have tasted the goodness of the word of God and the powers of the coming age, if they fall away, to be brought back to repentance, because to their loss they are crucifying the Son of God all over again and subjecting him to public disgrace. Land that drinks in the rain often falling on it and that produces a crop useful to those for whom it is farmed receives the blessing of God. But land that produces thorns and thistles is worthless and is in danger of being cursed. In the end it will be burned" (Heb. 6:4-8 NIV).

Third, he gives them *encouragement:* he points to *some signs of their growth.* "Even though we speak like this, dear friends, we are confident of better things in your case – things that accompany salvation. God is not unjust; he will not forget your work and the love you have shown him as you have helped his people and continue to help them. We want each of you to show this same diligence to the very end, in order to make your hope sure. We do not want you to become lazy, but to imitate those who through faith and patience inherit what has been promised" (Heb. 6:9-12 NIV).

Without going into details concerning this passage, its

implications for us should be obvious. First, does God expect less of us than he did of the people who originally read these lines? If spiritual progress was expected of them, do we seriously believe that he will accept spiritual stagnation in our lives? Who can be so naive? Second, will our failure to mature into the likeness of Christ not bring us under condemnation? God is no respecter of persons, and he will not permit in us what he censured in others like us. Third, what evidence of progress can we point to in our spiritual lives?

Through our living faith, God has saved us. We looked at some of the major implications of that fact in the previous chapter. Now we turn to an examination of heaven's challenge to Christians – the challenge of going on to maturity. A few basic facts about beginning and maintaining spirituality will be stressed. Most of them will be examined in greater detail in subsequent chapters of this volume. All are indispensable.

Burn Your Bridges Behind You

The first step to spiritual maturity is to *burn your bridges behind you*. What does this mean? It means cutting yourself off from the things and people of your pre-conversion life which would tend to draw you back to forbidden ways. This step reduces the likelihood of being seduced back into sin.

Your commitment to Christ means that you have died to the world. "Knowing this, that our old man was crucified with him, that the body of sin might be done away, that so we should no longer be in bondage to sin ... Even so reckon ye also yourselves to be dead unto sin, but alive unto God in Christ Jesus" (Rom. 6:6, 11). Being "dead

19

unto sin" simply conveys the notion of being unresponsive to sin. One who has genuinely repented of his past life is sorry about the things he has done against the will of God and is determined not to repeat them. It is this attitude which is the background for "burning your bridges," but it is not quite the same. Let me explain.

One could be genuinely sorry about (i.e., repent of) using profanity. His or her resolve never to use that sort of language again could be absolutely genuine. Suppose, however, that such a person continues to be with, eat with, and play tennis with people who use profanity constantly and from whom he or she originally picked up the habit? At the least, it would be very poor judgment. That person is deliberately staying in a situation which is going to make it easy to go back on the resolve about pure speech. This is the sort of situation in mind when speaking of bridges that need to be burned.

Visits with backsliding Christians often turn up the fact that they never completely cut themselves off from their pre-Christian past. Pornography ought to be burned, drinking friends should be abandoned, past partners in sexual sin must never be contacted again, jobs or business partnerships which compromise Christian principles should be given up. Until you are willing to burn these bridges behind you, the likelihood of using one of them to go back into sin (and away from Christ) will haunt your attempts at spiritual progress.

If you haven't done so already, give up the old people, places, and things which characterized your life prior to conversion. Carry through with the implications of your repentance, and make it clear to both God and men that you mean to be finished with sin.

Grow in the Knowledge of God

The second step to spiritual growth involves regular use of the Word of God. *Read and study your Bible daily.* There can be no advancement in the things of Christ apart from Holy Scripture. This is why we are instructed by the apostle Peter: "As newborn babes, long for the spiritual milk which is without guile, that ye may grow thereby unto salvation" (1 Pet. 2:2).

When one takes time to reflect on the things the Word is able to do for the child of God, he understands why it is so crucial to spirituality. Knowing and doing the words of Jesus will set one free from sin (John 8:31-32). The Word of God sanctifies (i.e., sets apart) people for the service of God (John 17:17). It is the only competent guide in right living (Psa. 119:11). Meditating on it equips him for doing good in service to God (2 Tim. 3:16-17).

Suppose you learned that a visitor from outer space came to our planet yesterday, made a speech in New York City, and departed with a promise to return someday. Furthermore it was reported that his speech was the most important ever made and will affect every person living on planet earth. Would you make an effort to secure a copy of that speech? Would you go over it carefully? Then how can we be so careless with our Bibles?

God has visited this planet in the person of Jesus Christ and has made known the significance of that visit through the pages of the Bible. He is coming again and will judge us by the things that are written in it. We neglect it only to our eternal peril! As J. B. Phillips has said of the New Testament: "Naturally, to any Christian these are the most important documents in the world. If we believe with our adult minds that we live on a planet visited by God Himself in human form, the record of His life and teaching and that of the movement which He began are of supreme importance to the entire human race" (Foreword to *Marshall's Interlinear Greek-English New Testament*, p. i).

Set aside a fixed amount of time every day for your personal study of the Scripture. Let your concern be to know not only the meaning of the passage in its context but also its application to your life. The scribes of Jesus' day knew the Law of Moses; they just didn't apply it to themselves (cf. Matt. 23). As you spend half an hour reading the Bible each day, keep your heart open, teachable, and humble so that what you are reading can produce a positive change in your heart and actions. You will not understand every detail of everything you read, but don't be discouraged by that fact. (Some suggestions on how to read and study the Scripture will be given in Chapter Six.) You will gain enough value from the most casual reading of this Holy Book to more than justify the time you spend with it. Then, as you continue to grow in knowledge, more and more of the deeper meanings of the Word will surface to your understanding.

Keep the Communication Line Open

The third step upward in your spiritual life is advocated in these words from Paul: *"Pray without ceasing"* (1 Thess. 5:17). Reading the Bible is allowing God to speak to you; praying is the means of communicating your thoughts and desires to him. This communication line needs to be open and in regular use. The apostle's counsel is that we should pray "without ceasing," i.e., regularly, continually, habitually. If you want to grow, it is a must.

Many Christians admit that prayer is not a vital and

regular part of their lives. In fact, many acknowledge that their prayer life is virtually non-existent. But how can one be a faithful follower of Christ without spending much time in prayer? At the inauguration of his public ministry, Jesus prayed while still standing with John in the baptismal waters (Luke 3:21). When pressed by crowds and the cares they urged on him, Jesus rose before daybreak to seek a solitary place for prayer (Mark 1:31-35). Before choosing the Twelve, Jesus spent a whole night in prayer about the matter (Luke 6:12). By one writer's count, the words "pray" and "prayer" are used at least 25 times in the brief record of his life in the four Gospels.

Most of us feel that we are so busy we cannot afford the time to pray. Our Savior had so much to do that he knew he would never get it all accomplished without prayer! Why can we not see the same necessity? Do we have hard decisions to make? Do our responsibilities ever pile up so high that it appears we will never see daylight again? When he was faced with similar situations, Jesus prayed. So should we.

Prayer, like profitable Bible study, requires discipline, forethought, and a workable schedule. Devout Jews set three specific hours of the day as "hours of prayer" (Acts 3:1) and observed them rigorously. The Roman centurion, Cornelius, imitated their practice and observed regular times of prayer (Acts 10:30). The use of the definite article (i.e., *the* prayers) in the Greek text seems to indicate something fixed, appointed, and regular. You will have to train yourself to such a practice, but the rewards of it are magnificent.

Some things in life are so difficult that they can be accomplished only through the special power of a believer's prayers. (Some special aspects of this part of our spiritual lives will be examined in Chapter Seven.)

Fellowship

Step four is this: *Share the fellowship of the saints.* The church is a *koinonia* (i.e., sharing in common, partnership) of faith, love, and good works. Every single member of the body of Christ needs the spiritual uplift that comes of being a part of a local church which has a positive and encouraging fellowship.

Take a close look at these familiar verses: "And let us consider one another to provoke unto love and good works; not forsaking our own assembling together, as the custom of some is, but exhorting one another; and so much the more, as ye see the day drawing nigh" (Heb. 10:24-25). Public assemblies of the church are times of mutual encouragement, stimulation, and spiritual challenge. Thus they are not to be neglected. In the particular context of the book of Hebrews, the writer says these meetings were the more urgent because of the great trials which were about to come upon those people. Since they would soon be tried severely by the persecution of Jewish people under Roman jurisdiction, these people needed to be attending these services and "storing up" strength against the unknown but threatening future.

By the same token, none of us knows what great trials may be ahead for him or her. Thus we dare not neglect the assemblies of the church while it is within our power to participate in them. Illness, injury, or some other unforeseeable turn of fortune may deprive us of the opportunity. Then we will need to draw on the strength we are building now.

Our fellowship must not be confined to our presence together at public assemblies of worship. A. B. Bruce has compared some churches to restaurants "where all kinds of people meet for a short space, sit down together . . . then part, neither knowing or caring anything about each other." Let us look for informal opportunities to be together as Christ's people to talk about the things of Christ and the church, to show an interest in each other's welfare, and to find ways to combine our energies for reaching the lost and reclaiming the erring. Small Bible study groups in homes, close friendships formed with believers, working together with Christians in church programs of service and outreach – all these constitute *meaningful fellowship* which stimulates spiritual growth.

True fellowship among believers – as opposed to constant bickering, backbiting, and witch-hunting – would make the church more attractive to non-Christians who need to hear our message. Paul warned: "But if ye bite and devour one another, take heed that ye be not consumed one of another" (Gal. 5:15). On the other hand, turning local churches into the places of warm fellowship God intended them to be will build up the church – and each individual member who shares in this sort of fellowship.

Win Others to Christ

The fifth step toward maturity in the faith is *soul-winning*. The ability and willingness of a Christian to share his saving knowledge of the gospel with someone else is the ultimate means to true spirituality. A pure life, study of the Scripture, prayer, and fellowship are designed to equip one for and move him toward the exercise of soul-winning. Becoming involved in taking the gospel to the lost will then insure his continued involvement in these activities.

About twenty years ago, *Time* magazine reported that churches of Christ were the fastest-growing religious group in America. Today we no longer have that distinction. Several studies within our fellowship have indicated that we are hardly growing at all. We are even losing ground to the rate of population growth. In a recent survey published in *Christianity Today,* churches of Christ have fallen from among the ten largest religious groups in America; we are now thirteenth in size. Do these statistics mean that we have lost our aggressiveness for souls? Have we become complacent about our responsibility to evangelize the world?

Evangelism is not the work of a select few in the church. It is something in which every Christian can and should participate. The sharing of Christ should be a natural part of the human relationships we have with family members, work associates, and friends. In fact, a term which in being used widely now is "friendship evangelism." Did we ever think we would evangelize people by treating them as enemies?

Atheists, pagans, misguided religious people, and erring Christians are not our enemies. They are victims of our enemy, and our role is to help rescue them from Satan's clutches. It is much easier for those people to respond positively to our attempts if they see us as their friends – people who really care about their spiritual welfare.

We are not mad at the communities we live in. We live among family, neighbors, friends, classmates, business associates, fellow-workers, and total strangers whose good will we can cultivate by allowing the beauty of Christ to be seen in us. With their goodwill, we can share the gospel with them. Many will hear and be saved. People will care about what we want to tell them if they know we care about them. Evangelism is just that simple.

It was stressed earlier in this chapter that some relationships with unbelievers must be ended at conversion. Yet this is not to say that the church should be so isolated as to become a "Christian ghetto." You don't have to compromise the truth to be friendly. You don't have to embrace falsehood to demonstrate honest concern for someone. You don't have to be immoral to be compassionate to some soul whose life is in ruins because of wickedness.

Sharing the gospel is still the most urgent business in the world. It is still God's "wisdom" to save men through the "foolishness" of the gospel message which has been entrusted to his people (cf. 1 Cor. 1:20-25). We must realize that non-Christians cannot be saved without the gospel and that the gospel will not be preached to those people by anyone except those who already have received it. "How, then, can they call on the one they have not believed in? And how can they believe in the one of whom they have not heard? And how can they hear without someone preaching to them?" (Rom. 10:14 NIV). We had best get about our task.

We must train and discipline ourselves as soldiers in an army to fight the battle for the minds and hearts – the souls – of men. (Some specific guidance in this area will be offered in Chapter Twelve.)

Conclusion

The current notion seems to be that spirituality is some mysterious thing which comes suddenly from on high

27

(usually through some powerful emotional experience) and transforms one into a spiritual giant overnight. The New Testament teaches that true spirituality comes about through gradual growth and changes brought about in us by the power of Christ. This is why no one of us has "arrived" spiritually; we are all seeking to walk with Christ more closely than ever before and to mold ourselves more nearly into his own likeness.

"Brothers, I do not consider myself yet to have taken hold of it. But one thing I do: Forgetting what is behind and straining toward what is ahead, I press on toward the goal to win the prize for which God has called me heavenward in Christ Jesus" (Phil. 3:13-14 NIV). I have cited these verses from the New International Version because of its rendering of the last part of this familiar statement from Paul. I like the idea that "God has called me heavenward in Christ Jesus." The principles of growth studied in this chapter are the ones that guarantee reaching the goal.

Some Things To Think About

1. Study Hebrews 6:1-12 in detail. What is the primary challenge of these verses? In what sense are we to "leave" the first principles of our faith?

2. What is the significance of "burning your bridges" when one becomes a Christian? How does this go beyond being sorry about the past? Show that genuine and complete repentance demands this radical step.

3. Why is the study of Scripture so vital to one's spiritual life? What method of regular study have you found most effective for you?

4. What does it mean to pray "without ceasing?" What are some of the things that hinder us from spending time in prayer?

5. What is the meaning of "fellowship"? How may Christians promote fellowship among themselves? Suggest some specific things that can be done among the believers where you are.

6. What motivates Christians to be evangelistic? Do you think we are as active in soul-winning as we should be? How will one's involvement in soul-winning help assure that person's continued purity, Bible study, prayer, and fellowship with the saints?

7. Spiritual growth is a gradual process. What are some of the signs of progress that one should look for in his or her life? What are the warning signals of possible apostasy?

Chapter Three

Look Who's On Your Side!

A few things in life may be "easy as falling off a log," but spiritual growth is *not* one of them! Going on to maturity in Christ is a daily struggle, a constant challenge.

For one thing, there are the constant attacks that Satan mounts against our faith. He is, after all, "a roaring lion ... seeking whom he may devour" (1 Pet. 5:8). Because of his skill as a deceiver of souls, we have to be on our guard constantly. "For our wrestling is not against flesh and blood, but against the principalities, against the powers, against the world-rulers of this darkness, against the spiritual hosts of wickedness in the heavenly places" (Eph. 6:12).

Then there are our own internal weaknesses and evil desires to contend with. "Each man is tempted, when he is drawn away by his own lust, and enticed" (Jas. 1:14). Have you ever lamented the fact that, whereas you want to do right and determine within yourself to follow the path of righteousness, you still yield to some chronic temptation? Paul acknowledged the same thing in his own experience when he wrote: "For I delight in the law of God after the inward man: but I see a different law in my members, warring against the law of my mind, and bringing me into captivity under the law of sin which is in my members. Wretched man that I am! Who shall deliver me out of the body of this death?" (Rom. 7:22-24).

Then, of course, there are false doctrines which will cause one to err from the truth. Anything which would compromise our faith and lead us away from Christ can result in eternal ruin.

It seems that so many things are working against us. Is there any hope of making it home to heaven?

Yes, there is hope! There is the sure and confident promise of God to the effect that *Christians are not alone in our struggle against sin.*

What with all the "spiritual hosts of wickedness" we must encounter, there would be no reasonable prospect of success in the Christian life if we were left to fight Satan in our own strength. I am no match for him! If I must do battle with him in my unaided strength, he will destroy me. But God is on my side, and his Spirit lives in me to strengthen me and give me the victory. Thank God for such a confidence!

First John 4 is a warning to Christians of the late first century about Satan and his onslaughts against them and the gospel they had embraced. The apostle warned his readers about the "spirit of the antichrist" (v.3) and the "spirit of error" (v.6). At the same time, he assured them of victory. Please read his statement of assurance closely, and pay particular attention to the reason underlying it. "Ye are of God, my little children, and have overcome them: *because greater is he that is in you than he that is in the world*" (v.4). The victory was theirs not by virtue of their strength but by the power of the Holy Spirit (i.e., "the spirit of truth," v.6) in them.

The confidence that John engendered in his readers by this great truth of the indwelling Spirit of God is the sort of confidence Christians need now. As we attempt to grow into the likeness of Christ, it will make all the difference to realize that we are not alone in the struggle. The wonderful truth of God's presence with us gives comfort, challenge, and incentive to holiness. In this chapter, we shall turn to Scripture and be impressed with this comforting and challenging doctrine.

The Holy Spirit Dwells in Christians

Many passages of Scripture affirm that the Holy Spirit indwells the saved individual. "But ye are not in the flesh but in the Spirit, if so be that *the Spirit of God dwelleth in you*. But if any man hath not the Spirit of Christ, he is none of his. *And if Christ is in you*, the body is dead because of sin; but the spirit is life because of righteousness. But if the Spirit of him that raised up Jesus from the dead *dwelleth in you*, he that raised up Christ Jesus from the dead shall give life also to your mortal bodies through *his Spirit that dwelleth in you*" (Rom.8:9-11). "Or know ye not that your body is a temple of *the Holy Spirit which is in you*, which ye have from God?" (1 Cor.6:19). "That good thing which was committed unto thee guard through *the Holy Spirit which dwelleth in us*" (2 Tim.1:14). "No man hath beheld God at any time: if we love one another,

God abideth in us, and his love is perfected in us: hereby we know that we abide in him and he in us, because *he hath given us of his Spirit"* (1 John 4:12-13).

We accept the fact of this indwelling by faith (i.e., taking God at his word). We do not presume to understand or explain the nature of such an indwelling – any more than we can understand or explain how our own spirits indwell our bodies.

The Spirit takes up his abode in an individual at the point of his salvation from sin. Look closely at Acts 2:38. "Repent ye, and be baptized every one of you in the name of Jesus Christ unto the remission of your sins; and ye shall receive the gift of the Holy Spirit." All those who obeyed the gospel on that occasion were promised the Holy Spirit. Furthermore, verse 39 makes it clear that the same gift would be given to all men of every race and time who would repent and be baptized for the remission of their sins.

There are no miraculous powers associated with this gift of the Holy Spirit. It does not enable one to speak in tongues or receive revelation in addition to that which has been given in the Word of God. This is simply his coming to take up an abode in the saved person for the purpose of strengthening him for spiritual life and struggles. It occurs in connection with one's obedience to Christ in baptism (cf. Acts 5:32). One does not receive this gift in order to make him a son of God but because he has become of child of God through the new birth of water and the Spirit. As Paul expressed it: "And because ye are sons, God sent forth the Spirit of his Son into our hearts, crying, Abba, Father" (Gal. 4:6).

So long as a Christian is attempting to walk in the light

of God's truth, the Holy Spirit continues to dwell within him to bring him to eternal life. If he begins to walk contrary to the truth, he "grieves" the Spirit (cf. Eph. 4:30). If he continues to engage in deliberate and unrepented sin, that person will fall from grace and "quench" the power of the Spirit of God in his life (cf. 1 Thess. 5:19). The Holy Spirit is not anxious to leave us nor is he looking for an excuse to do so. His interest is in helping us unto spiritual maturity, and he continues to strive for that goal until such time as we refuse the truth and turn away from our commitment to Christ.

What He Will Do For You

As to the function of the Holy Spirit as he indwells the Christian, several observations have been made already. Negatively, he does not bestow miraculous powers on people today. Supernatural gifts of the Spirit ceased to be available to mankind around the close of the first century, when the gospel had been fully recorded in inspired documents and adequately confirmed by signs and wonders. Neither does the Holy Spirit act to lead men to conversion by any direct means; the preached gospel is his instrument for convicting and converting sinners. What, then, does he do?

Gives Strength. The Holy Spirit *strengthens the Christian* to help him in overcoming sin. The Bible makes it plain that the Christian's ultimate salvation depends on achieving victory over Satan and the flesh. It lists the things which must be "put to death" (Col. 3:5ff). By what power are the children of God able to accomplish this great task?

All of us tell non-Christians who are struggling with

alcohol, drugs, or some other vice that "God will help you overcome this if you will obey the gospel and become his child." How will he do so? The believer who does his part in diligent watchfulness and prayer will receive strength from the indwelling Spirit to overcome sin. This is the promise of the Word of God. "If ye live after the flesh, ye must die; but if by the Spirit ye put to death the deeds of the body, ye shall live" (Rom. 8:13). It is not that we will feel his powers moving mysteriously in our beings. Rather, we know that we have his assistance in our spiritual strivings because the promise of such help is clear in the inspired Word.

Paul prayed for the Christians at Ephesus to the end that they might "be strengthened with power through his Spirit in the inward man" (Eph. 3:16). This was not a prayer for them to receive miraculous powers; it was a petition for their growth and strengthening. This same request can be made of heaven on behalf of children of God today, for this activity of the Holy Spirit did not end with the close of the first century.

Seals God's Children. The presence of the Holy Spirit is *God's seal* (i.e, branding mark) on his children. In ancient times, a seal was used to authenticate an object or to indicate its ownership. A ruler might press his seal into soft wax on the bottom of a decree; an artisan would affix his to the soft clay of his sculpture. The modern equivalent of such things would be a university's seal at the bottom of a diploma or a company's trademark stamped on its products. In a similar way, heaven has put a seal of identification and ownership on every saved man and woman. "Ye are sealed with the Holy Spirit of promise" (Eph. 1:13; cf. 4:30).

The imagery of this concept is quite beautiful. Special promises are made to the children of God in many places. They cannot be tempted above their ability to withstand (1 Cor. 10:13); all things will work together for their good (Rom. 8:28); angels minister for their sake (Heb. 1:14), etc. How are these special people identified? Is there some mark by means of which God's agents and heavenly ministers can distinquish Christians from other people? Indeed there is. The called and chosen people of God bear his seal in the presence of the Holy Spirit in them. "But if any man hath not the Spirit of Christ, he is none of his" (Rom. 8:9b).

Assists in Prayer. The Holy Spirit also *assists the Christian in prayer.* "And in like manner the Spirit also helpeth our infirmity; for we know not how to pray as we ought; but the Spirit himself maketh intercession for us with groanings which cannot be uttered" (Rom. 8:26).

There are many things that we know to ask for, because we feel a need for them or because the Bible instructs us to pray for them. These conscious and clearly expressed desires of the heart are offered in prayer, and Jesus intercedes and mediates for us in these matters. Sometimes our requests are not so articulate and go up to the Father in the form of sighs and groans from our burdened spirits.

Then there are the distresses and groanings of our hearts which are deeper still – so deep that they "cannot be uttered." The indwelling Spirit knows the situations and needs of that heart, and he makes intercession on its behalf. "He that searcheth the hearts (i.e., the Father) knoweth what is the mind of the Spirit, because he (i.e., the Spirit) maketh intercession for the saints according to the will of God" (Rom. 8:27).

Pledge of Salvation. The Spirit's indwelling is also an *earnest* (i.e., deposit, pledge) *of our final salvation.* "For indeed we that are in this tabernacle do groan, being burdened; not for that we would be unclothed, but that we would be clothed upon, that what is mortal may be swallowed up of life. Now he that wrought us for this very thing is God, who gave unto us the earnest of the Spirit" (2 Cor. 5:4-5). His presence with us is a guarantee that all of heaven's promises to the Christian will be fulfilled.

The word translated "earnest" here (Gr, *arrabon*) was used of a downpayment given on the receipt of merchandise as a guarantee that the rest of the amount promised would be forthcoming. It was also used of an engagement ring which served as a promise that a marriage would take place. The symbolism here is unmistakable. God's indwelling Spirit is his sure promise to us that we will share in a divine inheritance.

There may be many other things which are accomplished through the agency of the Holy Spirit as he indwells the saints and acts on our behalf. These four functions are specifically attributed to him in the written Word.

As to specific methods and means by which he accomplishes his works, we have no certain knowledge and speculation would be pointless. We accept the fact of their accomplishment by virtue of the promises contained in the Scripture and because of the fruit of the Spirit which is borne in the lives of God's people (cf. Gal. 5:22-23).

Of one thing we may be certain: *the Spirit of God will do nothing which is contrary to his revealed will contained in the written Word.* Thus we may dismiss as false the claims and doctrines of those who – while claiming the guidance of the Spirit – clearly walk in contradiction to the teachings of the Bible.

Comfort and Challenge

Great *comfort* comes to us in the knowledge that we are not left to our own devices in coming unto sanctification and eternal life. We are not alone!

When I was a little boy, a great deal of my time was spent with doctors and in bed. I was as weak and frail as a child could be. One day at school in what was probably the fourth grade, the class bully decided it was time for him to flex his muscles. So he came to my desk and said, "I'm going to beat you up at recess." What a prospect! The class weakling was going to be pummeled by a guy he had no hope of defying! But a friend sitting in the seat next to mine heard the threat and said, "You'll have to get by me to get to him." Since he was bigger and stronger than the bully, color began to return to my cheeks. Because he stayed with me during recess, I didn't have to take a licking.

This illustrates the point about the Spirit's presence with us. Satan is the bully of the human race. He is "a roaring lion ... seeking whom he may devour" (1 Pet. 5:8). Because we are so weak and spiritually helpless, he can break and defeat us at will. But we are not alone! The Spirit of God is our friend, companion, and defender, and "greater is he that is in you than he that is in the world" (1 John 4:4b). We don't have to be defeated, for he is with us to help, strengthen, and protect us.

There is also great *challenge* and incentive to personal holiness in the knowledge that we are indwelt by deity.

39

Our bodies are sacred and must not be defiled by sin. "Flee fornication. Every sin that a man doeth is without the body; but he that committeth fornication sinneth against his own body. Or know ye not that your body is a temple of the Holy Spirit which is in you, which ye have from God?" (1 Cor. 6:18-19a). The appeal of this passage is more profound than fear of disease, pregnancy, or disgracing one's family. Paul pleads for moral purity on the basis of the fact that our bodies belong to God and serve as temples for the Holy Spirit. "And ye are not your own; for ye were bought with a price: glorify God therefore in your body" (1 Cor. 6:19b-20). What greater challenge to personal purity could there be?

Conclusion

It is a bit frightening to realize what is expected of the people of God. The past must be put behind you. Your life must conform to that of the Son of God. You must face temptations on every hand and overcome them. You must serve the Lord and your fellow human beings, etc.

Is it possible to live this high and holy life? Can you do it? To be sure, you cannot do it by yourself. *But look who's on your side!* The Spirit of God is within you to strengthen, comfort, and aid you. He is willing to help you, and you can go on to maturity by his power in you.

This lesson closes with an appeal from Paul: "And be not drunken with wine, wherein is riot (excess, KJV), but be filled with the Spirit; speaking to one another in psalms and hymns and spiritual songs, singing and making melody with your heart to the Lord; giving thanks always for all things in the name of our Lord Jesus Christ to God, even the Father; subjecting yourselves one to another in the fear of Christ" (Eph. 5:18-21). The use of wine may make a man giddy, foolish, and irresponsible; the presence of the Holy Spirit has no such effect on an individual. To the contrary, his presence makes us strong, stable, and dependable in spiritual things. He enables us to become the people God calls us to be.

Some Things To Think About

1. How does one's attitude toward a contest (e.g., baseball game) affect his performance in that contest? Is it reasonable to think that one's attitude toward living the Christian life will affect his performance in this spiritual contest? Examine the first several verses of 1 John 4 in this connection.

2. How do we know that the Spirit of God dwells in Christians? When does he take up his abode in the children of God? Under what circumstances will he leave a Christian?

3. Human beings are spiritually weak, and Satan has had the power to tempt and defeat us prior to conversion. Why are things different following our salvation? What does the indwelling Spirit accomplish on our behalf?

4. The Holy Spirit "seals" the children of God. Explain this beautiful concept. What function does such a sealing serve?

5. Although Christ is our only *mediator* with the Father in heaven (cf. 1 Tim. 2:5), the Bible teaches that the Holy Spirit is an intercessor on our behalf. Study Romans 8:26-27 carefully.

6. What is the significance of the Holy Spirit as heaven's "earnest" to the Christian?

7. What *comfort* and *challenge* do you see in the doctrine of the indwelling Spirit of God? How does your knowledge of this truth encourage you in your efforts to go on to maturity?

Chapter Four

MORE THAN CONQUERORS

The New Testament abounds with expressions of joyous confidence in salvation. "I know him whom I have believed, and I am persuaded that he is able to guard that which I have committed unto him against that day" (2 Tim. 1:12b). "If God is for us, who is against us? ... Who will separate us from the love of Christ? shall tribulation, or anguish, or persecution, or famine, or nakedness, or peril, or sword? ... Nay, in all these things we are more than conquerors through him that loved us" (Rom. 8:31-39).

This sense of spiritual security is sometimes lacking in children of God today. These people sing "I am Bound for the Promised Land" and "When We All Get to Heaven," but deep down inside they wonder whether they are going to heaven or not. Such people live in spiritual agony – wondering from one moment to the next about their salvation. Some even become mentally ill because of an overwhelming sense of insecurity. These people need the consolation which comes with the realization that they are God's children and heirs, that they are secure in his grace.

The Lord does not want his people to live in doubt and insecurity. To use the language of Hebrews 6:18, he desires us to have a "strong encouragement" about our eternal prospects. Particular parts of the Bible were written for the express purpose of creating such a confident attitude among Christians. For example, "These things have I written unto you, that ye may know that ye have eternal life, even unto you that believe on the name of the Son of God" (1 John 5:13).

The theme of this chapter is that the child of God can know he is saved and can rejoice daily in his confidence in Christ. The development of this sort of spiritual security is an important part of going on to maturity. Assurance of salvation is a fortress of strength against Satan. It brings power and purpose to our spiritual lives; it adds zeal and vitality to the service you offer the Lord. In the absence of such assurance, one lives a dispirited, sad, and heavy-hearted Christian life. So confidence in Christ is not merely "a nice thing to have" but a necessity for victorious living.

How Can I *Know* I Am Saved?

Many Christians have posed this question: *How can I know I am saved?* They have read Bible statements about the confident knowledge of salvation. They have heard other Christians express their confidence about eternal life. They would like to share the same assurance others have expressed to them – but do not know how to come by it.

There are really only *three possible answers* to this question.

First, it would be possible to hold that an individual cannot be sure he is saved. Someone of this mind would answer the question "How can I know I am saved?" by saying that only God knows the spiritual status of men and that he will reveal it to us only at the Judgment. The best this person could do in affirming his confidence about the future would be to say something like, "I hope I am saved" or "I want to be saved" or "I'm trying to be saved"; he could never make the confident affirmation of Paul in saying, "There is laid up for me the crown of righteousness, which the Lord, the righteous judge, shall give to me at that day" (2 Tim. 4:8a). This individual would have to judge others' statements about their confidence in salvation as impetuous claims without biblical substance.

This answer and the attitudes it entails are clearly wrong. The apostle John plainly said that he had written his epistle to ordinary Christians like us so they could *know* they had eternal life. If there was a means by which they could be confident of their salvation, there is a means by which we can be confident of ours. God is not a respecter of persons.

Second, some contend that people can know they are saved by the way they feel about the matter. In fact, this is probably the most frequent "evidence" offered by religious folk as the basis for their spiritual assurance. Yet, the Word of God warns us repeatedly about being guided by our feelings in spiritual things. "There is a way which seemeth right to a man," wrote Solomon, "but the end thereof are the ways of death" (Prov. 14:12).

We dare not try to determine our spiritual status before

the Almighty by some physical or emotional feeling. Conscientious Christians burdened with illness or family problems have been known to say, "I just don't know anymore whether I am saved or not." On the other hand, people who are ignorant of the will of God but who are happy and carefree of disposition "know" they are saved. This is not how one's spiritual condition can be known. Feelings are too volatile and unstable, whereas salvation is an abiding relationship with God which persists through all the ups and downs of a lifetime.

Third, it can be argued from Scripture that God has designated a way by which a person can determine objectively whether or not he is saved. Take a close look at 2 Corinthians 4:16 – 5:10. Although "our outward man is decaying" and there are causes for discouragement at times, Paul insisted that he and his readers remained confident of "an eternal weight of glory" (4:16-18). In other words, our feelings cannot tell us whether or not we are saved. And, yes, it is possible to know that "we have a building from God, a house not made with hands, eternal, in the heavens" (5:1).

But how? How can we know we are saved? The answer is given in verse 7: "For we walk by faith, not by sight." Faith is not a subjective leap to be taken when all else fails. Biblically speaking, faith is taking God at his word; it is accepting his testimony on a matter and being sure on the basis of God's promise.

To illustrate, imagine a prisoner being offered a pardon. He takes and reads the document but is so overwhelmed that he is dazed by the news. Someone asks, "Have you been pardoned?" He answers, "Yes." "Well, do you *feel* pardoned?" the questioner asks. "No, I don't; it is so sudden," says the man. "But if you don't feel pardoned, how can you know you are?" "Oh," he says, as he points to the document in his hand, "this tells me so." The Bible is God's document of pardon to his people, and assurance is possible by believing it.

The Bible Tells Me So

In the first chapter of this book, God's plan for saving people from their alien sins (i.e., sins committed prior to conversion) was studied closely. From that study, it was learned what an individual must do to become a Christian. He must learn the gospel, believe it, repent of his sins, and be baptized in the name of Jesus Christ unto the remission of his sins. If you have complied with these requirements, you have been forgiven of your sins committed prior to that time, added to the spiritual body of Christ (i.e., the church), and made a child of God. How do you know? The Bible says it is so.

You can know whether you are a Christian or not in the same way you can know that you are an American citizen or a married person. If you have met certain stipulations of law, you are an American citizen. If you have complied with the laws governing marriage, you are married. If you have obeyed the will of God about salvation, you are a Christian. It is just that simple. This is something you can know – not guess about. It does not depend on your feelings – whether good or bad – but on the objective Word of God and your conscious response to it. You know you are a Christian, because the Bible tells you so.

The crucial concern of this chapter, however, has to do with those of us who are Christians already. How can we know that we are *still* saved? Doesn't the Bible teach that children of God can fall from grace? How can I be sure that I have not fallen away?

Here is a simple, direct, and biblical response to these questions: (1) If you are sincerely concerned about the matter, the likelihood is that you have not fallen from grace. (2) In any case, there is a sure way to determine your spiritual status before the Lord by means of the teaching of the Word of God. Let's look more deeply at these two affirmations.

Yes, the Bible teaches that a man or woman who has been saved *can* fall away from Christ and be lost. Paul warned: "Wherefore let him that thinketh he standeth take heed lest he fall" (1 Cor. 10:12). Peter wrote of this possibility among Christians: "For if, after they have escaped the defilements of the world through the knowledge of the Lord and Savior Jesus Christ, they are again entangled therein and overcome, the last state is become worse with them than the first" (2 Pet. 2:20). Yes, people can turn back on their commitments to Christ and be lost.

But the teaching of the Bible to the effect that saved people *can* fall away and be lost should not be interpreted to mean that they are *likely* to do so. Or, to put it another way, the *possibility* of apostasy is not the *probability* of apostasy. Saved people can enjoy the confidence of knowing that they are saints of God bound for heaven by means of two tests.

First, *check the condition of your heart.* How do you feel about the sins you commit? Are you humble enough to admit them and repent of them? Or are you defensive and proud? Is there some sin that you love more than Christ and are deliberately permitting to remain in your life?

Christians still sin. The fact that we have been born again does not mean that we cannot do wrong any more. It means that we have a different attitude toward the wrongs we commit. "If we say that we have fellowship with [God] and walk in the darkness, we lie, and do not the truth: but if we walk in the light, as he is in the light, we have fellowship one with another, and the blood of Jesus his Son cleanseth us from all sin. If we say that we have no sin, we deceive ourselves, and the truth is not in us. If we confess our sins, he is faithful and righteous to forgive us our sins, and to cleanse us from all unrighteousness. If we say that we have not sinned, we make him a liar, and his word is not in us" (1 John 1:6-10). This is a very important passage dealing with our topic and should be studied closely.

Notice how important *attitudes* are held to be in these verses. If we love God, we must hate sin. This means that, while we do not deny that we still commit sin, we confess them and allow the blood of Jesus to cleanse them from our souls. We know that sin grieves God, and thus it grieves us, too. It is only if we sin and refuse to repent of what we have done that we fall from grace.

A while earlier in this chapter, it was said: "If you are sincerely concerned about the matter [of falling away], the likelihood is that you have not fallen from grace." That statement should be clear now. The very fact that a Christian recognizes that he could be lost and is honestly concerned about his right relationship with God indicates that he is spiritually sensitive, that he is not involved in living a life of deliberate sin. It is only when we sin willfully (i.e., regularly and/or impenitently) that Christians fall from grace. "If we deliberately keep on sinning after we

49

have received the knowledge of the truth, no sacrifice for sins is left" (Heb. 10:26 NIV). So long as our hearts are tender and penitent – though our flesh may be weak – God holds us secure in his grace.

Second, *look for evidences of growth in your spiritual life*. Are you increasing your knowledge of the Word of God? Is your faith growing stronger? Do you have more self-control over your emotions, tongue, and deeds? Are you being kind and helpful to your brothers and sisters in Christ?

The very qualities listed above – along with virtue, patience, and love – are listed by Peter in 2 Peter 1:5-7. We often refer to them as the Christian Graces. After enumerating them and urging his readers to possess them in increasing measure, the apostle wrote: "For if ye do these things, ye shall never stumble: for thus shall be richly supplied unto you the entrance into the eternal kingdom of our Lord and Savior Jesus Christ" (2 Pet. 1:10b-11). Look at the promise made here: Do these things and you will never fall!

So here are the two tests from the Word of God by which a Christian can examine himself as to whether he is still saved. Have you eliminated all deliberate (i.e., conscious, known, and unrepented) sin from your life? Are you consciously doing things which will increase the measure of Christ-like traits in your life? If your truthful answer to these two questions is "Yes," you are saved, secure, and heaven-bound. The Bible says so. You simply need to believe what the Word says and rejoice in your assurance. If the answer to either question is "No" for you, you are not spiritually secure and you need to do some things immediately.

Saved By His Life

"But God commendeth his own love toward us, in that, while we were yet sinners, Christ died for us. Much more then, being now justified by his blood, shall we be saved from the wrath of God through him. For if, while we were enemies, we were reconciled to God through the death of his Son, much more, being reconciled, shall we be saved by his life; and not only so, but we also rejoice in God through our Lord Jesus Christ, through whom we have now received the reconciliation" (Rom. 5:8-11).

Pay particular attention to the argument which is developed in this Pauline statement about salvation. Having been sinners and enemies of God at one time, we have now been reconciled unto God through the death of Jesus. "Much more," however, we are now going to be saved by his life. What does this mean? Moses Lard makes these comments about the verses in question: "In his life-state, or living state, subsequent to his death, Christ consummates all the provisions of salvation, and in person superintends the work. In this way he brings it to a successful end, and so saves us by his life, or by being alive. There is no other way apparent in which Christ's life can have the effect to save us."

The salvation that Christ died to make possible for us is completed in his ongoing work for our sakes. Since a dying Christ reconciled us, surely a living Christ will keep us from divine wrath. Since he went to the cross for us when we were his enemies, surely he will save us now that we are his friends. Since he overcame the initial difficulty in saving us (i.e., death), surely he will overcome all other obstacles which might get in the way now.

Heaven wants us to share in and enjoy the full benefits

of salvation. God is doing his part in making it possible.

Conclusion

In an era of fear, doubt, and uncertainty, you can have the spiritual security of knowing that you are protected by divine grace. By means of the simple tests provided in this chapter, you can "Examine yourselves to see whether you are in the faith" (2 Cor. 13:5 NIV). Having passed these tests, you can have confident assurance about your eternal welfare. Such assurance rests upon the firm promises of God in Holy Scripture.

It is an important step toward spiritual maturity to realize that you are able to live with unwavering confidence rather than nervous misgiving. The Bible is God's document of pardon to you, and assurance is possible by believing the precious promises of the Word of God. So rejoice. Be confident. Live victoriously in Christ!

Some Things To Think About

1. A sinner needs rebuke which will bring him to repentance; a saved person needs assurance that God has truly pardoned his past sins and is anxious to help him get safely home to heaven. Yet many sinners are comfortable, and some Christians are troubled. Contrast the biblical statements of confidence in salvation with the disposition of some believers.

2. What is the theme of this chapter? Why is confidence in Christ so important to the attainment of spiritual maturity? What is the result of its absence?

3. What are the three possible positions one might take

about the possibility of knowing that he or she is saved? Evaluate each. Which is biblical?

4. How can one be absolutely sure that he is a Christian? You may wish to review some of the materials in the first chapter of this book in formulating your reply to this question.

5. Two tests are given in this chapter whereby a Christian can know whether or not he is secure in the grace of God. Examine each carefully, and explain the significance of each. Do you agree that these tests are (1) biblical and (2) adequate for their intended purpose?

6. Study Romans 5:8-11 very carefully. How does the argument developed by Paul in these few verses contribute to the thesis of this chapter?

7. What is the difference between confidence and arrogance? How does the Christian keep his confidence about salvation from degenerating into arrogance?

Chapter Five

Life in a
Sex-Oriented Society

In 1979 *Playboy* celebrated its 25th anniversary. The very fact that national TV carried a one-hour special into American homes in prime time to mark the occasion tells something about the powerful impact of the sexual revolution which has occurred during that quarter century.

The Chicago Board of Aldermen adopted a resolution of congratulation to Hugh Hefner for having created a "magazine which is the product of talented journalists, editors and artists, and which is imbued with Mr. Hefner's *Playboy* philosophy stressing the fundamental importance of the individual, freedom of expression, free inquiry and academic achievement in education, separation of church and state and the protection of the will of the minority …" As columnist Patrick Buchanan said of that resolution, it is "beyond satire."

We Christians had best face the fact that our Bible-

55

centered values are no longer "mainstream" to the American way of life. We live in a cultural context of godlessness and anti-Christian philosophy. Nowhere is this quite so apparent as in the sphere of sexual ethics.

Global society is sex oriented and sex saturated. From billboard advertising to comedians' monologues to best-selling fiction, sex is the dominant theme. There can be no sports event without large slices of cheesecake for the audience; it begins with strutting majorettes and twirlers at halftimes of the high school football game and continues to the Dallas Cowboy Cheerleaders. Popular radio stations which cater to teens sponsor wet T-shirt contests among their female listeners, and nude dancers perform in clubs across the country every day. And these are some of the milder affronts to Christian sensibilities!

Here is an ad which was run in two Denver newspapers: "Single professional woman, 34, interested in meeting an intelligent, healthy male for purpose of becoming pregnant. No financial obligations, although open to discussing relationship if desired." Carolyn Myer received over 200 responses to her ad within two weeks. A 17-year-old male homosexual made national headlines when he challenged school officials for the right to bring his boyfriend to the senior prom; the American Civil Liberties Union considered taking his case into the courts for him on constitutional grounds.

The Alan Guttmacher Institute of New York has done what most researchers consider the most definitive study of sexual trends among young people in the '80s. According to their study, 12 million of today's 29 million teenagers are having sexual intercourse. Nearly half the boys and one-third of the girls between the ages of 15 and 17 are sexually active. One of every ten teen-age girls becomes pregnant each year in the United States. Contraceptives are easy to obtain without parental consent; the consensus opinion among teens is that "everybody is doing it"; abortion is an easy and increasingly acceptable "solution" if there is an unwanted pregnancy.

I am not advocating a return to Puritanism, with its drab clothes and ridiculous strictures. Puritanism upheld an oppressive sexual ethic which surely created a great deal of unhealthy aversion toward a subject treated positively in Scripture. What I am advocating is a return to a biblical ethic of sexuality as an alternative to the pagan attitudes and behavior of our sex-oriented society.

While many of the appeals to be made in this chapter are directed to younger Christians, they are of relevance to believers of all ages. One thing is for sure: *Spiritual maturity entails moral purity.* Therefore this chapter is necessary to the development of the theme of this book.

Positive View of Sex in the Bible

Many people have been led to think that the Bible presents a totally negative view of sexuality. Nothing could be farther from the truth.

God created the race male and female. When he united the first man and woman, he indicated that their sexual union was to be an important part of the total oneness which he desired for them. Quoting the Old Testament record with approval, Jesus said that it was God's will that husband and wife be "one flesh" in marriage (Matt. 19:5; cf. Gen. 2:24).

That there is nothing unholy about the physical relationship of marriage is evident from passages such as this:

"Let marriage be had in honor among all, and let the bed be undefiled: for fornicators and adulterers God will judge" (Heb. 13:4). The Holy Spirit has made it plain that sex within marriage is wholesome, beautiful, and good. At the same time, he has made it plain that sex outside of marriage is degrading, ugly, and sinful. There is a difference between *love* and *lust*.

The sexual relationship of marriage has been ordained of God as a means by which a man and woman can express their love for and commitment to each other in an intimate manner. Sex is not only for the begetting of children but is also for the delight of two people in each other as companions. It is right for young people to look forward to the time when they will be able to experience this ecstasy.

Not to wait until marriage for sexual experience is not only to rebel against the God of heaven but also is to thwart the joy which could have come with sexual experience. People who experiment with sex before marriage cannot appreciate it for the beautiful joy it is, for the God who has created them has made it inevitable that feelings of shame will spoil the experience for them.

It is not wrong for a young person to feel sexual stirrings. It is a natural part of growth. Hormones cause certain sensations which cannot be controlled with conscious effort. Something you see or hear by chance may excite some sexual feeling. It is wrong, however, to purposefully excite these feelings and to exploit them. Pornography, masturbation, petting, and all similar deliberate stimulations of sexual excitement have no place in the life of a person who is trying to maintain purity before a holy God.

Remember that purity is not the absence or denial of passion; it is the proper directing and ordering of that passion. Remember also that sexuality is only one aspect of your total personality, and people whose attraction to and use for each other involves sexual desire as the primary factor will have a woefully inadequate basis for love and permanence in their relationship.

WHEN PEOPLE TURN AWAY FROM GOD

What is behind the moral degeneration of our time? What has unleashed the floodgates of indecency and brought about a situation where plays, movies, and novels glorify unprincipled living and make it appear desirable? What has turned us into a sex-oriented society where "casual sex" (i.e., participation in illicit sex with hardly a thought about it) is both accepted and expected among high school students?

Some say that two world wars, Korea, and Vietnam are responsible. Others blame it on poverty and overcrowding in the nation's big cities. Still others attribute it to the Pill, a lack of sex education in public schools, or some other factor. These are *not* primary causes of character erosion.

Hear the Word of God diagnose the cause of moral decay: "Because that, knowing God, they glorified him not as God, neither gave thanks; but became vain in their reasonings, and their senseless heart was darkened. Professing themselves to be wise, they became fools ... " (Rom. 1:21-22). People have turned away from God. They have refused to acknowledge him, his Word, his authority over their lives. "And even as they refused to have God in their knowledge, God gave them up unto a reprobate mind, to do those things which are not fitting" (Rom.

1:28). Men and women have turned to sexual impurity because they have turned away from God.

In the eighth century B.C., the prophet Hosea delivered this stinging indictment of his own people in Israel: "They sacrifice upon the tops of the mountains, and burn incense upon the hills, under oaks and poplars and terebinths, because the shadow thereof is good: therefore your daughters play the harlot, and your brides commit adultery" (Hos. 4:13). Israel first turned away from the true God to idols. The man of God predicted that, as a result of their religious apostasy, promiscuity and whoredom would become commonplace. It came to pass then, and it has happened again. Over the past few decades, theological liberalism took over the seminaries and pulpits of the Western world. Promiscuous sex is commonplace now, and avowed homosexuals have been ordained to the clergy of several denominations.

Until the authority of the Bible is recognized by men, the reestablishment of morality in our world will remain only a dream. Until prophetic preaching is heard by people in the pews, there will be no reversal of present trends to even grosser immorality. Until people who claim to believe and follow the Bible demonstrate their profession through rigorous separation from the things of the world, "righteousness" will remain merely an archaic word in the contemporary vocabulary.

A call for repentance and right living must be sounded forth again. As the prophets of old, we must identify sin for what it is and reprove the works of darkness. We must warn men of the terrible consequences which come of disobedience and generate a true hunger and thirst for righteousness.

Embracing a Christian Lifestyle

In a sex-drenched culture where the playboy/playgirl philosophy is dominant, exactly what would it involve to adopt Christian purity as a way of life?

Purity of Heart. First, one must commit himself to purity of heart. Since behavior is the product of the thoughts, desires, and preoccupations of the inner man, the Bible requires that we guard our thoughts. "Keep thy heart with all diligence; for out of it are the issues of life" (Prov. 4:23). Specifically, the Lord warned that adultery and fornication result from allowing one's heart to become defiled (Matt. 15:19). Peter wrote of lewd men "having eyes full of adultery" (2 Pet. 2:14a); their hearts were so obsessed with impure thoughts that they saw every person of the opposite sex with a lustful appraisal (cf. Matt. 5:28).

The sex-oriented society of our time has conspired to destroy purity of heart and to create a situation in which everything is seen and sold through an appeal to sex fantasies. Of course there are hard-core pornographic books, magazines, and movies which are allowed to the public. How I wish that Christians could never be looked at through the same eyes that have seen this sort of mind-polluting filth. Yet an increasing percentage of people in our society have subjected themselves to its influence. Demonstrate enough moral virtue never to attend such a movie or leaf through such a magazine. It will have such a corrupting impact on your heart that mother or sister, father or brother, Sunday School teacher or Christian friend will thereafter be subject to an impure gaze which makes even these good people the potential objects of evil thoughts. You may fight against them, but once you have allowed your mind to be touched by this filth, it will be impossible to keep such thoughts out of your mental processes entirely.

The same influence can be had on one's heart by the more respectable and subtle media of certain PG movies, popular television programs, and many commercial advertisements appearing on TV and in printed media. To judge from what is shown on TV, for example, one would think that all human activity occurs in semi-tropical climates among men and women clad in swim wear. Sexual innuendo is the rule in dialogue written for situation comedies aired in prime time for young viewers.

A study done for *Public Opinion* magazine by Linda Lichter, Robert Lichter, and Stanley Rothman received a great deal of attention when it was published in January of 1983. Interviews with 104 members of the media elite – reporters, editors, script writers, film editors, and television producers – turned up the following facts: 93% said they seldom or never attend religious services; four out of five did not consider homosexual relationships wrong; 54% said adultery was not immoral; 87% said women should have the unrestricted right to abortion. Are these people trying to promote their positions on these and similar issues via their media? "Two out of three believe that TV entertainment should be a major force for social reform," the report said. "According to television's creators, they are not in it just for the money. They also seek to move their audience toward their own vision of the good society."

Not to be outdone by the programs, sponsors take their turn with the same formula. Soft drinks are sold by breathless girls running from the ocean in bikinis to get a favorite cola from a cooler on the beach. Men are prompted to buy hair products or after shaves by scenes of men who are unable to keep girls' hands off them after using certain brands. Magazines and newspapers print pictures of near-nude bodies of both male and females in order to sell tanning lotion or exercise courses.

Is it any wonder that purity of heart is a difficult attainment? Our culture practically worships sex through its visual media. It has created a situation where "having eyes full of adultery" is portrayed as the norm.

If we are really serious about purity of heart, we will have to guard ourselves against the types of assaults against virtuous thoughts which have been mentioned above. We will have to discipline ourselves against purposefully seeking out such literature or attending such movies or viewing such TV programs. The Christian who feeds on such things cannot maintain his or her spiritual health.

Pure Speech. Second, one must give attention to clean speech. People who are really committed to Christ-like living must use "sound speech that cannot be condemned" (Tit. 2:8). Such persons might well adopt the prayer of David: "Let the words of my mouth and the meditation of my heart be acceptable in thy sight, O Lord, my rock, and my redeemer" (Psa. 19:14). In the point made earlier concerning purity of heart, attention was focused on visual factors which both reveal and mold us. Now we turn to the important matter of the spoken word.

The Lord himself called attention to the revealing nature of speech. He said: "Out of the abundance of the heart the mouth speaketh" (Matt. 12:34). The individual who uses God's name in irreverent ways reveals his lack of respect for deity; the one who employs suggestive language and likes to tell off-color stories lets it be known that his heart is impure. The person who uses his tongue to speak of Jesus, to pray, and to praise the Lord is likewise showing the orientation of his heart.

Believers are supposed to restrain our tongues (Jas. 3:1ff) and put away "shameful speaking" from our mouths (Col. 3:8). In a sex-oriented society, we have to guard against picking up slang and repeating jokes that make some indecent reference. "Let no corrupt speech proceed out of your mouth, but such as is good for edifying as the need may be, that it may give grace to them that hear" (Eph. 4:29).

One of the things which merits concern in this regard is the thoughtless repetition of sexually explicit lyrics from many popular songs. This sort of thing has a teaching power, a mind-shaping ability. To deny that the music we listen to and sing affects our thinking and behavior is to say that God had no purpose in requiring the use of psalms, hymns, and spiritual songs in worship. To say it doesn't affect us is to disavow the feelings we have all had in singing "God Bless America" or "The National Anthem" in the context of a patriotic gathering.

The sensual lyrics of modern music serve to desensitize people to spiritual things and to make us more tolerant of the next step down and away from the high standard of purity which has been set in Scripture.

Illicit love affairs have been stock-in-trade for country music over the years. Recently we were told that "Heaven's Just a Sin Away" by the Kendalls. Barbara Mandrell sings these words to a married man: "If loving you is wrong, then I don't want to be right." Conway Twitty is notorious for his sexually explicit lyrics. He took a song which had already been released as a rock tune and did his own country version of "I Want a Lover With a Slow Hand." Some of the most popular songs on rock stations during the same period have been these: "Nobody Does it Better," "Do Ya Wanna Make Love, or Do Ya Just Wanna Fool Around?", and "Ecstasy is When You're Lying Down Next to Me." "Jack and Diane," a song by John Cougar, has these lyrics: "A little ditty about Jack and Diane;/ Two American kids growing up in the heartland./ Jack, he's gonna be a football star./ Diane debutante back seat of Jacky's car ... / Diane sitting on Jack's lap. He got his hands between her knees./ Jack, he says, 'Hey, Diane. Let's run off behind the shady tree;/ Dribble off those Bobbie Brooks./ Let me do what I please.'" Suggestive? Hardly. *Explicit!*

These few songs are not departures from the norm of modern music. They are mainstream and are aired time after time on the most popular stations in the country. Their attachment to sexual themes and their promotion of an anti-Christian morality is evident.

I am not opposed to writing, performing, or hearing music. Few people are any more inclined than I to turn on a radio as soon as I get in a car or to turn on a stereo system when at home. So I am hardly in position to call for stereo smashings or record burnings. What I am pleading for is *discrimination*. Since music carries values and helps establish social norms, children of God have to be careful about paying their money and lending their influence to songs which bear an unholy message.

Modest Dress. Third, in a sex-oriented society, Christians will have to be particularly careful about modest clothing. The human body is not evil. In the sinless state of the original couple in Eden, their nakedness was neither shameful nor embarrassing. When sin entered, however, nakedness took on an altogether different meaning. The very first consequence of their sin was that "the eyes of them both were opened, and they knew that they were naked; and they sewed fig-leaves together, and made themselves aprons" (Gen. 3:7). What had once signified innocence was now connected with shame. So it has been in the eyes of God since that day (cf. Gen. 9:21-27; Neh. 3:5; Rev. 3:18).

The current push toward nudity and the uninhibited baring of flesh is a part of mankind's rebellion against God. Fashion designers and trend setters are doing all they can to promote it. Clothes are advertised as "daring," "sexy," and "sensuous." The attitude held and promoted by the fashion establishment appears to be the one expressed by a former fashion editor at *Harper's Bazaar,* Nan Kempner. "I can't wait for summer," she said, "for anything that shows more of me is divine."

In the introduction to this chapter, the Dallas Cowboy Cheerleaders were mentioned. They are without question the unabashed sexpots of the NFL, and television cameramen covering the football games have made them a prominent part of the nation's weekend viewing fare. CBS sports producer Chuck Milton said, "The audience deserves a little sex with its violence." Not to be outdone by football, baseball teams now have skimpily clad girls chasing foul balls and sweeping off the bases. And professional basketball teams have rushed to get into the act, too. In setting guidelines for the cheerleaders he was looking for, a promotion director for one NBA team said, "We're gonna put them in the skimpiest uniforms possible that won't be obscene and won't get us arrested."

Yet Christian parents become indignant if anyone dares suggest that their daughters are indecently dressed or inviting lust when they are members of cheerleading squads which imitate the "professionals" from Dallas or bare their buttocks in majorette and twirling costumes. Do lecherous eyes and lewd remarks not shame these young people or their parents? Are Christians so perverse of heart that we think we can encourage our children to be sexpots?

Then, during the warmer months of the year, modesty is challenged by our American fetish for sun and water. Now swimming is certainly one of the best exercises for the human body, and there is nothing intrinsically evil about swimming or sunbathing. Both are wrong, however, when they are done is public places or in mixed company. There is no sensible person who thinks that a woman is modest when she reclines in a chaise lounge on the side of a swimming pool in the middle of an apartment complex and is wearing only a bikini. A hard look at some man staring at her hardly compensates for putting oneself in position for him to see what he is seeing; turning her head away when he makes some suggestive remark about her does not make her innocent in the matter. The same principle applies to men as well as women. The bronzed and muscled male who parades in a pair of swim trunks on the beach or the knock-kneed fellow who gets some sun by mowing his yard in nothing but a pair of gym shorts is immodest. If this isn't true, it is simply impossible for a male to be immodest. The next step for him is nudity.

The human race cannot return to the innocence of Eden by returning to the nudity which prevailed before sin entered the world. To the contrary, we compound our sinfulness by defying the will of God in following the standards of dress which have been set by a sex-oriented world.

Chaste Behavior. Fourth, living in a world which aspires to a style of behavior which is patently evil, a Christian must exhibit chaste behavior.

In Galatians 5:19-21, two of the words used in Paul's catalog of "works of the flesh" are designed to warn Christians against behavior that is vulgar and lewd. The first is "lasciviousness" (Gk, *aselgeia*); it refers to conduct which follows an "inclination to sensuality ... indecent conduct" (Arndt and Gingrich) or actions which involve "indecent bodily movements, unchaste handling of males and females" (Thayer). The second is "revellings" (Gk, *komos*); it refers to "carousing, revelry" (Arndt and Gingrich) and "merrymaking with music and dancing" (Liddell and Scott). The modern equivalent to these terms which comes to mind most quickly are certain types of modern dance. If ever there were "indecent bodily movements" and "indecent conduct" among humans, they are cases in point. The movements of any number of them are obviously in imitation of sexual intercourse.

The fundamental appeal of dancing is sex. That is why it is such a popular form of entertainment in our sex-oriented society – and that is precisely why a Christian cannot participate in it. The suggestive movements and unchaste touching of two people on a dance floor arouse desires in a normal person which cannot be satisfied without additional sin being involved. It is beyond my powers to imagine why a person who has made a commitment to be like Christ would defend and/or participate in the modern dance.

Sexual Purity. Fifth, if you are determined to follow

Christ in this sex-oriented world, you will have to maintain your sexual purity. In the case of an unmarried young person reading this book, this means that you must maintain your pre-marital virginity. Or, if it is too late to speak to you of virginity, you must repent of your fornication, allow a gracious God to forgive you, and draw upon his strength to live the life from this time forward that you should have been living already. In the case of married persons reading the book, this means that you must be faithful to your legitimate companion. There is only one person in all the world who can be the focal point of your sexual desires and activities — your husband or wife.

Based on a comparison of birth certificate information with population statistics, the incredible fact emerges that one out of every ten teen-aged girls in the United States becomes pregnant. One million of these girls are between 15 and 19 years old, but about 30,000 are below 15. One-third of all abortions involve teen-agers.

For every ten unmarried, pregnant teen-agers, three will give birth, six will have abortions, and one will have a miscarriage.

The State of Georgia has the third-highest teen-age pregnancy rate in the country — one in eight teen-age girls becomes pregnant each year. The Georgia Obstetrical and Gynecological Society said the failure to use contraceptives because of misleading or false information from other teen-agers is the principal cause of the pregnancies. Wrong! It is the lack of moral integrity among people that is the cause of illicit pregnancies, not the lack of birth control information and devices! The cure for what ails our sick world is not free pills and diaphragms. The cure is respect for God and adherence to his ethic of sexuality.

Casual sex is commonplace among high school and college students. The parents of these young people may be naive and trusting; they may still take their children to Sunday School and worship regularly; they may have never felt it necessary to teach their children anything specific about sexuality from a Christian point of view. The high school and college students of our sex-oriented society have more information on sex than they let their parents know about. If that information and the values attached to it did not come from Christian sources, it is highly unlikely that they have a biblical code of behavior in mind. Thus it becomes someone's duty to appeal to them to avoid fornication and to try to point them to a positive view of sexuality in the context of a Christ-centered value system.

Extra-marital sexual activity is increasingly common among people of all age levels. It seems to mean very little that some people have pledged themselves to sexual fidelity to each other until death. Is there any way to appeal to these people which will move them to honor their commitments?

Paul made an appeal for sexual purity from the strongest base possible. "The body is not for fornication," he said, "but for the Lord; and the Lord for the body" (1 Cor. 6:13). Paul's argument is to the effect that the bodies of Christians belong to the Lord, thus believers must seek his glory in everything. "Know ye not that your bodies are members of Christ? Shall I then take away the members of Christ, and make them members of a harlot? God forbid ... Flee fornication ... he that committeth fornication sinneth against his own body. Or know ye not that your body is a temple of the Holy Spirit which is in you, which ye have from God? and ye are not your own; for ye were bought with a price: glorify God therefore in your body" (1 Cor. 6:15-20).

A Christian appeal for you to maintain sexual chastity is not based on the possibility that you might contract venereal disease. Neither is the concern so much that you might "get somebody pregnant" or bear a child out of wedlock. The fear is not that you might get trapped into an early and bad marriage. It is not that you might be found out by your husband or wife and lose your home. The Christian plea for sexual purity is for people to take their allegiance to Christ seriously. Honor the fact that you belong to him. Don't let our pagan world influence you to think that the thrill of fornication is worth giving up Jesus to experience. You belong to Christ, and the Spirit of God dwells in you. Don't desecrate your body by using it as an instrument for unrighteousness.

In this sex-oriented world you face every day, you will be tempted repeatedly to give up your sexual purity. If you come to your wedding day as a pure man or woman, it will be because you have guarded yourself from sin – not by chance. If you keep your commitment of sexual fidelity to your husband or wife, it will be because you choose to do so – not because you will not have the opportunity to have an affair.

Conclusion

We have the divine standard for our lives on earth in the Bible. Although some people seem to be of the opinion that sex was discovered in the twentieth century, heaven has taught us the right ethic of sexuality in that holy book. A pure heart, clean speech, modest dress, chaste behavior, and sexual purity are the five key elements to the adoption of a lifestyle that is Christian in this sex-oriented age. No one will find himself or herself better off by violating the divine standard and refusing the lifestyle to which God has called us.

"We are a temple of the living God; even as God said, I will dwell in them, and walk in them, and I will be their God, and they shall be my people. Wherefore come ye out from among them, and be ye separate, saith the Lord, and touch no unclean thing; and I will receive you, and will be to you a Father, and ye shall be to me sons and daughters, saith the Lord Almighty. Having therefore these promises, beloved, let us cleanse ourselves from all defilement of flesh and spirit, perfecting holiness in the fear of God" (2 Cor. 6:16b–7:1).

If you plan to go on to maturity in Jesus, you will have to take this matter of purity seriously. Whether you are a teen-ager or a grandfather, life in our sex-oriented world is a special challenge to godliness. We will have to adjust our values and discipline our lives to meet the challenge.

Some Things To Think About

1. Distinguish Puritanism from Christianity with regard to their respective views of human sexuality. Read the Song of Solomon. What is its theme? What view of sexuality is presented?

2. How do you account for the moral degeneration of our time? What will change the attitudes and behavior of men and women about such things?

3. Many things are at work today to destroy purity of mind. Secure a copy of the day's newspaper for your city,

and examine the movie ads and TV schedule for today. What appeals are made to sexual themes in the movies and TV programs the people of your city are watching today?

4. What are some of the places and circumstances which tempt people to use their tongues for lewd purposes? What are some of the popular songs of today which contain suggestive lyrics? Is the trend toward sexual explicitness in music greater or less today than when this book was written?

5. Define *modesty*. Is it possible to establish a general rule for distinguishing modest clothing from that which is immodest?

6. Do you agree that dancing is an unchristian form of entertainment? Why do so many people defend dancing? What are some of the newer dances which are particularly offensive to Christian standards of righteousness?

7. What problems are created for their later lives (especially in marriage) by people who participate in premarital sex? What are some of the usual consequences of extra-marital sex?

Chapter Six

Living Spiritually: The Bible

There is no other book in the world like the Bible. One may find in its pages beautiful poetry, exciting historical drama, moral challenge, fascinating personalities, inspiration, comfort, etc. Yet none of these accounts for its uniqueness.

The Bible is unequaled in all literature because it is *the very Word of God to mankind*. It is the special revelation of the mind of deity, telling of the redemption of sinful men by the grace of God. "All Scripture is God-breathed and is useful for teaching, rebuking, correcting and training in righteousness, so that the man of God may be thoroughly equipped for every good work" (2 Tim. 3:16-17 NIV).

Nothing in the realm of human responsibility is so urgent as one's obligation to know and do the will of God. As the prophet Jeremiah said, we humans are not capable of finding our own way through the maze of life. "O Jehovah, I know that the way of man is not in himself; it is not in man that walketh to direct his steps" (Jer. 10:23). We need an intelligible revelation from God to give light and direction for our steps. As God speaks to us through his word, that need is met. "Thy word is a lamp unto my feet, and light unto my path" (Psa. 119:105).

For the Christian who desires to grow spiritually, the Bible is "food for the soul." Peter likened the divine revelation to milk for newborn babes (1 Pet. 2:2). The writer of Hebrews said the Word of God was not only milk for younger believers but also "solid food" for those who are more mature (Heb. 5:11-14). One never outgrows his need for the Bible. Whether you are a new convert or a veteran soldier of the cross, you need to continue feeding on the Word of God every day of your life. For you to neglect regular and systematic Bible study is both to diminish your possibilities for growth and to increase the likeliness of sin in your life. It is an inescapable fact that a lack of Bible knowledge dries up the roots of godliness (Hos. 4:6; cf. Psa. 119:104).

For all this, however, some Christians read their Bibles just as they read newspapers – skimming off only the most superficial facts. To get at its very heart – and in order for it to take hold of your heart – *the Bible has to be studied as a textbook*. Careful reading, underlining, note-taking, re-reading, research, and constant review are as necessary for learning Scripture as for learning American history. This may sound demanding and tedious, but it is the type of study which is absolutely necessary for your growth to spiritual maturity.

In this chapter, we shall try to discover a practical and

workable system of studying the Word of God. Our goal is to introduce some tools and techniques to you which you can begin to use immediately in the mastery of Scripture.

Basic Convictions About the Bible

Before looking at a Bible study method, let us examine some basic convictions which one must bring to his study of Scripture in order to profit from it. There are four key terms to be looked at just here: perfection, authority, power, and intelligibility.

Perfection. To claim that the Bible is perfect is to say that it is the complete will of God revealed to humankind. Insofar as the work of revealing the divine mind to us, God has finished the job through Christ.

In Old Testament times, God was gradually revealing his will to men (cf. Isa. 28:10). When the Old Testament was completed, the total process of revelation was still not perfected. The people were still looking for the prophet like Moses (Deut. 18:15-18); they were still anticipating the law which God had promised to write on the hearts of men (Jer. 31:31-34). Then Jesus came and promised that the revelation of God's will would be completed through the work of his apostles (cf. John 16:13). The Holy Spirit came to accomplish that work, the promise was fulfilled, and the Word of God stands complete.

No new revelation has been added since the first century of this Christian Age, and none will be given until Jesus appears again. This means that the Bible we have in our possession is the sum total of God's revelatory work in history, and all that humankind can know of his will is contained therein.

Authority. Jesus Christ has been given "all authority

in heaven and on earth" (Matt. 28:18). He has spoken himself with that full authority, and he has spoken through his apostles and prophets. The written words of Jesus and his ambassadors constitute authoritative Scripture. Thus Paul could write: "If any man thinketh himself to be a prophet, or spiritual, let him take knowledge of the things which I write unto you, that they are the commandment of the Lord" (1 Cor. 14:37).

As students of the Bible, we must respect its authority – both in what it says and in what it does *not* say. It is incorrect to ask "Where does the Bible forbid so and so?"; the correct question is "Where does the Scripture authorize it?" We must have a "thus saith the Lord" for everything we believe, teach, and practice in religion. This is the only way to respect the authority of the Word of God.

Power. God's words have always been able to accomplish their intended purposes. He spoke the universe into being; he upholds the created order by the power of his word; Christ stilled storms and raised the dead by his words. Surely the *written* words of God are no less powerful than his oral ones. In fact, we are prone to consider the words of men to be the more binding and powerful when written (e.g., contracts) than when delivered orally.

Yet men seem to have been dissatisfied with the written Word of God throughout history and have wanted something more. For example, the rich man in torment wanted a messenger from the spirit world to go warn his brothers back on earth. Abraham told him, "They have Moses and the prophets; let them hear them." When the rich man protested that that would not be enough, the reply came, "If they hear not Moses and the prophets, neither will they be persuaded, if one rise from the dead" (Luke 16:27-

31). Today we not only have Moses and the prophets (i.e., the Old Testament) but also the words of Christ and the apostles (i.e., the New Testament). The wild and far-fetched claims of men to personal experiences of God and the revelation of new truths to them by such experiences are false.

We must put our total confidence in the power of the all-sufficient revelation given in Scripture. It has the power of God unto salvation inherent in itself (Rom. 1:16).

Intelligibility. Some people – even some Christians – do not study the Bible because they are under the false impression that it cannot be understood. But Scripture is intended for everyone and not for just a handful of trained experts and church leaders. *All* believers are to allow the Word of God to dwell in them richly (Col. 3:16). Paul wanted his writings read among all the brethren for the sake of their instruction and edification (1 Thess. 5:27). If the Bible cannot be understood, then either God *could not* give a verbal message his creatures could understand or else he *would not* do so. To say the former is to impeach his power; to say the latter denies his goodness.

The Bible is understandable in the translations we have available to us. In fact, today's student of the Bible in English is in a most favorable position to read and interpret Scripture – probably in a more favorable position than anyone since the first century, when Spirit-guided inter-preters were available.

Most people who have ever studied the Bible have done so by means of a translation. The knowledge of Hebrew, Aramaic, and Greek is helpful for technical study of Scrip-ture but is not necessary for one to study, know, and obey the essential truth of God for his salvation from sin and victorious Christian living. Jesus and the earliest Christians used a Greek translation of the Old Testament which had been made around 250 B.C. It was known as the Septuagint and is terribly defective in many places. Yet our Lord and the early church were confident that it could be used for the teaching of truth and for the saving of souls. Today we have a host of translations available to us. Not all of them have been made as carefully as others, and one needs to be aware of the strengths and weaknesses of whatever version he chooses to read. But I know of no English translation which is so bad that it obscures the truth to the degree that a sincere student could not learn from it what to do to be saved. Frankly, my fear is not so much that someone will use the "wrong translation" as it is that he will simply ignore the Bible altogether. When I find any man reading any Bible, there is hope that he can be brought to Christ for salvation. The fact that we have a number of English translations means they can be compared on any given text and checked for accuracy by this means.

Yes, there is a lot of controversy over translations. Which is best? What version is most faithful to the original texts? Which one reads most fluently in English? What translation will more people be using where I study and teach? Which one suits my personal tastes best? All these are relevant questions to one's choice of a Bible for personal study, but this is ultimately a *personal choice* to be made by each of us. I dare not try to tell you which translation of the Bible you must use. It is more important to try to teach you an attitude and method which will enable you to get the most out of whatever version you select for use.

The Elements of Bible Study

Turning to the technique of effective Bible study, there are three fundamental elements which need attention. Let us look at each in turn.

A Time and Place. The first essential is *a fixed time and place* for your study. Assuming that you believe the Bible to be the very Word of God to man and have a sincere desire to grow in spiritual maturity by means of it, you must become very definite and specific about attaining your goal. This means setting a fixed time and place for the first session.

Don't wait for the right time to show itself or for "spare time" to surface. Satan will win over your holy resolve to be a serious student of the Bible if you begin so haphazardly. You may need to get up earlier, stay up later, or pay some such high price for the time you need. You will probably need to do nothing more than give up some TV, newspaper reading, or telephone visiting in order to secure *30 minutes a day.* This is the ideal amount of time at the start of your new program of study. Don't "burn yourself out" by trying to stay with it for a very long time, but do give yourself enough time to really accomplish something. Thirty minutes will be about right.

You will find it helpful to use the *same time every day.* Your study time comes to be a part of your regular routine.

It is also a good idea to *use the same location each day.* A desk is ideal, but any table or other writing surface will work. Keep your study Bible and other tools for research at that spot, so they will be handy and available to you without having to waste time gathering them. Using the same place for your Bible study each time will have the psychological effect of helping you begin your concentration more quickly in order to get about the business at hand.

The Right Tools. Second, you will need *the proper tools for Bible study.* Now don't get frightened at this point, for I am not talking about hundreds of dollars and dozens of books. You already have most of the things you need, and the others can be gotten inexpensively at most any discount department store. There are five basic books required for your study: (1) a Bible, (2) a loose-leaf notebook and paper, (3) a Bible concordance, (4) a Bible dictionary, and (5) a good English dictionary.

Be sure to use a Bible with clear print, margins wide enough for notes to be made, maps of Bible lands, and center-column (or marginal) cross references.

Which version of the Bible should you use? As already indicated, this is a matter for personal choice. Whichever translation you choose, be aware of its strengths and weaknesses. Here are some of the relevant facts about a few of the primary Bibles in use today.

Many people still use the *King James Version* of 1611. Its high literary style and many archaisms (cf. Acts 19:38; 21:15; 28:13; 1 Thess. 5:14; James 2:3, *et al.*) have decreased its usefulness for people of our time. One wishing to stay with the King James Version would be wise to use the updated *New King James Version* (New Testament 1979, Old Testament 1982); it preserves as much of the traditional King James language as possible while modernizing most of the archaic words and streamlining the punctuation.

The *American Standard Version* of 1901 has long been recognized as an excellent translation for close textual study. It is as close to a "literal" (i.e., word-for-word) translation as one can come by. While this is a strength for some purposes, it is a weakness for others. It results in some very awkward English readings which can be misleading. *The New American Standard Bible* (1971) improves many of these readings and is a very useful version.

The Revised Standard Version (Old Testament 1946, New Testament 1952) has become the standard version for "mainline Protestantism" in America. Most commentaries and reference works in English use it. The handling of passages such as Genesis 12:3, 18:18, 22:18, and Isaiah 7:14 in this version has caused many conservative students to be highly critical of the Revised Standard Version.

The New International Version of 1978 has gained wide acceptance among conservative students because of its handling of the passages noted above which were problematic in the RSV. It is unquestionably the most readable translation in English. At times it tends to interpret as well as translate a text (cf. 1 Cor. 7:36-39).

My personal recommendation is that you use one of the translations just listed as a primary study text. Whichever you prefer reading most, it would be wise to have one or more of the others at hand for comparative reading whenever you are doing serious study. It is amazing how much insight one can get into a passage just by comparing the versions. [Note: For a detailed examination of various translations, see Jack P. Lewis, *The English Bible From KJV to NIV* (Grand Rapids: Baker Book House, 1981), or Sakae Kubo and Walter F. Specht, *So Many Versions,* rev. ed. (Grand Rapids: Zondervan Publishing House, 1983).]

Why do you need a loose-leaf notebook? You just can't

learn as much if you don't write, make notes, jot down questions for further study, etc. The exact use of the notebook will be explained later when we get to "Some Methods of Bible Study."

An unabridged concordance lists all the verses in the Bible in which a particular word is found. It is especially useful for finding how a word is used throughout Scripture and in finding additional information on certain subjects. A concordance does not define words or furnish explanations; it serves only to locate words in their biblical context. Be sure to get a concordance which is geared to the version you have chosen as your primary study text.

A Bible dictionary supplies historical, geographical, literary, and theological data concerning a subject at hand. For example, a concordance would point one to the occurrences of the word "Pharisee," but a Bible dictionary would tell him something of the origin of this Jewish sect, its peculiar beliefs, its influence at various periods of history, and why Jesus was often critical of them. One of the best Bible dictionaries is by J. D. Douglas, ed., *The New Bible Dictionary*, 2nd ed. (Eerdmans). A briefer dictionary which has been edited by a member of the church of Christ is Reuel Lemmons, ed., *The New Smith's Bible Dictionary* (Doubleday).

The last item suggested, an English dictionary, is of limited value – since the Bible was not originally written in English. But you should have one handy for the sake of reference.

Please notice that commentaries are omitted here. This is a deliberate omission which is designed to encourage you to work directly from the text on your own rather than take the view of someone who has already done your work for you. If you come across a particularly difficult text, consult commentaries for whatever help they may provide. Don't be afraid to take issue with a commentary, however, for it is not inspired.

A System. Third, you will need *a system of study which is practical.* Just opening and reading your Bible will not do the job. You need a systematic approach to the Bible which incorporates several important features. In this connection, be sure to examine the next section of this chapter very carefully. It outlines a tested method of study which has been useful to many people. If you do not have a system of study already, it certainly beats the one you are using now!

Some Methods of Bible Study

The Five-R Method

The method of Bible study I recommend to new Christians who are beginning their systematic mastery of the Word of God (or to older ones who have neglected to develop their own method already) is called the "Five-R Method." It is best suited to a textual study of the Bible, and this seems to be the most profitable sort of study for most people. Each step in this approach begins with the letter "R" (for ease of remembering) and proceeds in a logical way to the understanding and application of Scripture.

Step One: *Read.* After choosing the book to be studied (e.g., Luke), begin each day's session by reading a paragraph, chapter, or other complete thought unit in your study Bible very carefully. It will be helpful to read the same verses in another translation or two and to take note of any significant difference of reading. Then read the section once more in your original version.

Step Two: *Reflect*. Now that the text has been read closely, begin asking yourself questions about it. What words or terms are unclear to you? Check your Bible dictionary or English language dictionary to clear them up. Who is the speaker or writer? To whom are the words addressed? Why would this writer say these things to his original readers (i.e., try to get a feel of the historical setting)? What appears to be the theme of the section you have read? Is there a key term which recurs through it? Here you may wish to use your concordance or Bible dictionary, along with your cross references, to read other passages which are similar or which discuss the same subject. Finally, ask yourself how this text relates to the needs and circumstances of your own life.

Step Three: *Repeat*. Here is where the loose-leaf notebook comes into use. Enter a heading in your notebook for the passage you have been studying, and state the central message of the text in your own words. You may wish to outline the verses, jot down some helpful cross references, record some information you found in the Bible dictionary that throws light on the passage, or state a goal for your own spiritual life in view of the text. If you cannot write down the theme of the verses you have studied in your own words, you don't understand the text yet. (Note: See Appendix A of this book for a sample of the sort of notebook entry you might make on a passage.)

Step Four: *Recite*. Pick out the key verse/statement of the passage you have been studying, and memorize it. This is important to the process and must not be omitted. Although some call memorization "kid stuff," we all memorize things we consider essential – Social Security numbers, addresses, football plays, etc. What is as important as the Word of God? Surely David was talking about his habit of memorizing Scripture when he wrote: "Thy word have I laid up in my heart, that I might not sin against thee" (Psa. 119:11).

Step Five: *Request.* As you come to the end of your half hour with the Bible, pray for the Father to help you incorporate some specific lesson from the text you have been studying into your life. Pray for him to help you in your daily attempts to know and do his will more perfectly. "But if any of you lacketh wisdom, let him ask of God, who giveth to all liberally and upbraideth not; and it shall be given him" (Jas. 1:5).

Prepared Systematic Studies

Some persons like to study through the Bible by means of outlines, background information on books, identified themes, etc. One needs to be cautious about using prepared guides, for the author may reflect personal biases or lead one to accept certain false views. If you choose this method, select a study guide which is minimal in the amount of its commentary on the text and whose goal is to let the text speak for itself. If this approach appeals to you, you may want to examine my *Book-By-Book Study of the Old Testament* and *Book-By-Book Study of the New Testament* (20th Century Christian).

Word/Theme Study

Many people enjoy studying the Bible through particular words or themes. This can be a very profitable way to master the Scripture, too. Select a key word or theme of the Word of God, and use your concordance and Bible dictionary to trace it through the Old and New Testaments.

Record key facts and findings in your notebook; underline important verses, and make notes in the margins of your Bible; memorize verses and/or statements which you find especially useful.

Character Study

The study of the Bible through some of its key personalities is also a very rewarding approach. Read and study all the Bible passages which refer to a given figure. If you decide to try this method, begin with Barnabas, Priscilla and Aquila, or some other lesser figure before attempting the mass of material which can be found on Paul or Peter. As you study, what events and experiences from the lives of these people teach you the most valuable lessons for your own life?

Conclusion

A young lady picked up a book and began to read it. She soon laid it aside, however, saying it was too dull and difficult. Later she met a man, dated him, and came to love him very much. She subsequently learned that he was the man who had written the book she had once tried to read without success. Then she went back to it and began reading it again, and this time she read it from cover to cover. Why the difference in the two readings? Now she knew and loved the author! If you know and love Christ, you cannot but want to read and study this book – the Bible.

In order to grow spiritually, you must discipline yourself to the diligent and regular study of Scripture. There is no shortcut to maturity, and the demanding work of Bible study cannot be eliminated. Our "American way of life" accents recreation and relaxation. While a certain amount of leisure and play are good, too much of it makes us soft and lazy. And while few people have ambitions beyond their capacity, they often have ambitions beyond their discipline. The capacity for grueling application to a task is lacking in too many of us.

Learning the Bible requires a discipline which will hold you to the task when it is tedious, cut out other things for the sake of a spiritual priority, and carry through on the basis of habit rather than impulse or mood.

What about you? Will you apply yourself to the mastery of the Word of God for the sake of going on to maturity?

Some Things to Think About

1. This chapter insists that the Bible ought to be studied as a *textbook*. What justification is there for such a view? What are its implications? Do you agree?

2. Define each of the following terms as it is used of the Scripture: perfection, authority, power, and intelligibility.

3. Which translation of the Bible do you use for personal study? Why did you choose it? What are its strong points? What are its weaknesses?

4. What tools of Bible study are recommended in this chapter? What function does each serve? Which ones are you familiar with by virtue of use? Which ones are available to you?

5. What method of Bible study have you used most effectively? What is your opinion of the "Five-R Method"? Would it be more worthwhile than your present method?

6. Self-discipline will be discussed at some length in a

later chapter of this book. Why is this virtue so important to Bible study? Is every page of Scripture as "exciting" as every other? How effective are you in holding yourself to regular study of the Word of God?

7. What is the most helpful thing you have learned from this chapter? What difference do you expect it to make in your personal study habits?

Chapter Seven

LiviNq SpiRiTuAlly: PRAYER

In Chapter Six, the importance of a daily period of quiet and unhurried devotional time was stressed. The object of such a period is not Sunday School preparation, required study for a high school or college Bible class, or anything of that kind. It is to nourish and strengthen your soul through drawing near to God. One author has said: "There is no path to holiness but in being much and long alone with God."

If you should miss your daily study time once or not spend as much time in it on a given day as you do ordinarily, that does not mean that your spiritual life is a failure. But if you do not even have such a time in your schedule, or if you go for days at a time without using it, something is wrong with your relationship with God. You are neglecting him and depriving your soul of the nourishment it needs for growth.

You need a definite time and place, so you can be alone and free of distraction. You need a humble and seeking spirit, one which yearns for God and growth. You need a system of Bible study such as the "Five-R Method." And you need to learn *the power of prayer* in the life of a child of God.

The place of public and united group prayer is not to be minimized. Such prayer is a vital part of our public worship of the Lord. But the need of personal and private prayer is the topic to be emphasized in this chapter. Among Christians who really desire to grow into the likeness of Christ, prayer assumes an importance which can hardly be overstated.

David, the sensitive man of God in the Old Testament, knew the value of prayer. "Morning by morning, O Lord, you hear my voice; morning by morning I lay my requests before you and wait in expectation" (Psa. 5:3 NIV). One wonders if the neglect of this morning habit was a part of his radical drift away from God for a time in his life. Our Savior taught us to make place for prayer in our lives through his example in the matter. "And in the morning, a great while before day, he rose up and went out, and departed into a desert place, and there prayed" (Mark 1:35). The apostles, whom Jesus taught to pray (cf. Luke 11:1-4), insisted they would not take on so much responsibility in the Jerusalem church that their prayer lives would have to be neglected. "We will continue stedfastly in prayer, and in the ministry of the word" (Acts 6:4).

Our period of daily devotional time with God must give attention to both elements of a two-fold fellowship with deity: Bible study and prayer. This lesson will seek to challenge you to a regular, purposeful, and effective prayer life. What a crucial matter this is in going on to maturity!

The Privilege of Prayer

Prayer is a unique privilege because *it gives one the opportunity to be like Jesus.* From the cradle in Bethlehem to the tomb at Jerusalem, his life was punctuated with prayer. He prayed as he performed signs (John 11:41-42), in privacy (Matt. 14:23), on the eve of his death (Matt. 26:36-44), and even on the cross as he was dying (Luke 23:34). He prayed for his friends, family, believers, future followers, and even enemies!

During the time of his earthly ministry, his disciples were so impressed by his prayerfulness that they asked to be taught to pray. "And it came to pass, as he was praying in a certain place, that when he ceased, one of his disciples said unto him, Lord, teach us to pray, even as John also taught his disciples" (Luke 11:1). Surely we, too, see prayer in the life of our Lord and feel compelled to learn how to pray that we may be more like him.

The privilege of prayer is also evident in the fact that *it is an effective means of fighting Satan.* Satan is our spiritual foe, and we must resist him with all the means available to us. Jesus taught us to pray: "And bring us not into temptation, but deliver us from the evil one" (Matt. 6:13). I wonder how many unnecessary temptations have been faced by Christians during the past week because we did not pray this petition daily? Then, in the face of those temptations we must face, prayer is again the key to escape. Too many of God's people embrace temptation when it comes instead of fleeing to God in prayer. An old, familiar song says:

Take the name of Jesus ever
As a shield from every snare;
If temptations round you gather,
Breathe that holy name in prayer.

When someone is inviting you into sin or when you are about to lose your temper and sin with your tongue, *pray!* You need not drop to your knees and say the prayer aloud. Stare into the eyes of the person provoking you, resolve not to lose your head, and say silently, within your heart, "Oh God, help me. I am so weak, but I do not want to sin!" Or, if it is a situation you have no business staying in, turn and walk away from it – praying every step of the way for God to keep you from sinning and to help you keep away from such people and situations in the future.

An old adage has it that "Satan trembles when he sees the weakest saint on his knees." It must be so. Satan's power to tempt is no match for God's power to strengthen and shield his own. When a saint is praying he is "plugging into" divine power which will help assure him of the victory over temptation. Regular prayer is a fortification of the soul against Satan.

We should also remember that *prayer is the way to get things from God*. This is not to say that we can be selfish in our prayers. If we pray with wrong motives and try to use God for our self-seeking purposes, our requests will be fruitless (cf. Jas. 4:3). But we would be foolish not to use prayer in the way the Bible encourages us to for the sake of receiving blessings that we need. James chided some first-century Christians by writing: "Ye have not, because ye ask not" (Jas. 4:2b).

In his Sermon on the Mount, Jesus taught us to call on the Father in heaven as a son would call on his earthly father. "Ask, and it shall be given you ... Or what man is there of you, who, if his son shall ask him for a loaf, will give him a stone; or if he shall ask for a fish, will give him a serpent? If ye then, being evil, know how to give good gifts unto your children, how much more shall your Father who is in heaven give good things to them that ask him?" (Matt. 7:7-11).

In the brief prayer Jesus taught his disciples (Luke 11:2-4), there are four requests in three verses. And Paul wrote: "In nothing be anxious; but in everything by prayer and supplication with thanksgiving let your requests be made known unto God" (Phil. 4:6). We struggling Christians are needy people, and prayer is our means of getting the things we need.

Finally, prayer is a wonderful privilege because *it is the means to close fellowship with God.*

Imagine a close friendship, with the two people living in the same community. Then one of them moves away. For a time, there are frequent communications. Phone calls are made, letters are written, and visits are exchanged. After a while, though, one of them begins neglecting communication, and the two people drift apart. There are new friends and other interests, and the former friend is all but forgotten. The same sort of thing happens in spiritual matters. When you are not praying regularly, you and God are drifting apart. After a while, he seems very far away. There is only one cure, and that is to get back in regular communication with him through prayer.

CONDITIONS of ACCEPTABLE PRAYER

As we attempt to develop effective prayer lives, there

are certain things to be kept in mind in order to make our prayers effective.

Selflessness. First, *we must pray without calling undue attention to ourselves.* One of Jesus' criticisms of the Pharisees was that "they love to stand and pray in the synagogues and in the corners of the streets, that they may be seen of men" (Matt. 6:5b). One who leads a public prayer is in danger on this point, of course. But there is even danger of violating the Lord's prohibition on this point by our private prayers in public settings. For example, Christians should certainly give thanks for their food in restaurants as well as at home. But should a display be made of it?

Should we announce or give the appearance of boasting over our private devotions? Our private prayers should really be *private,* and prayer must never become a matter of display.

Sincerity. Second, *we must not allow our prayers to degenerate into mere formality.* Jesus warned against using "vain repetitions" in prayer (Matt. 6:7). For example, think of the way we sometimes pray at meals or at bedtime. Unless we guard against it, these prayers can be a series of set words and cliches which have no real meaning to the person saying them: "Bless the sick and afflicted the world over," "We pray not for ourselves alone but for all those for whom it is our duty and privilege to pray," "Bless thy ministering servants everywhere," "Bless this food to the nourishment of our bodies and our bodies to thy service." There is nothing wrong with these expressions – so long as they express the sincere and conscious sentiments of the one saying them. Most of them are so trite and threadbare that they are in danger of being vain repetitions for us to use thoughtlessly.

Faith. Third, *we must pray with the full confidence of faith in God.* How do we know the Father is hearing us? How do we know he will answer us according to his wisdom? Scripture is our promise and guarantee that our requests are being received by a receptive Father. God is a liberal giver, and we must take our requests to him "in faith, nothing doubting" (Jas. 1:5-6). To attempt to pray without confidence in God's promise to hear and answer is to guarantee failure.

Submissiveness. Fourth, *we must always pray according to the will of God.* "And this is the boldness which we have toward him, that, if we ask anything according to his will, he heareth us: and if we know that he heareth us whatsoever we ask, we know that we have the petitions which we have asked of him" (1 John 5:14-15). We certainly cannot ask for something which we know to be against the righteous will of deity. Because we often do not know all that is involved in our requests or whether those things asked for would truly serve the purposes of God in our lives or not, we must make all our requests contingent upon the will of God (cf. Luke 23:43).

Penitence. Fifth, *we must be living lives of obedience to God in order for our prayers to be effective with him.* "For the eyes of the Lord are upon the righteous, and his ears unto their supplication" (1 Pet. 3:12). A Christian loses his power in prayer if he is not surrendering himself to the will of God or is impenitent over any sin he has committed. It is not sin but impenitence that destroys a Christian's prayer rights (cf. Acts 8:22).

Cooperation. Sixth, *we must be willing to do whatever is necessary on our part to have our prayers answered.* For example, it is foolish to pray for health and not take care of oneself; it is foolish to pray for the church and not support her every good work; it is foolish to pray for the lost and not try to teach your friends who are not Christians.

THE HOW of PRAYER

After all the things discussed above have been said – after an individual has a keen desire for an effective prayer life and after one has set aside a time and place for prayer – many Christians still need teaching as to the very procedure of prayer. *How* does one pray? By means of an acrostic with the word "pray," an attempt will be made to answer this practical question.

Praise. Allow the first letter of the word to remind you to *praise* Father, Son, and Holy Spirit in your prayers.

The very qualities of the divine nature elicit praise and adoration from the Christian. In Psalm 145, David extols the Lord for his goodness and power. "Every day will I bless thee," he said, "and I will praise thy name for ever and ever" (v.2). The reasons for this attitude are his greatness, mighty acts, great goodness, mercy, etc. You and I worship and pray to the same God David did, and our reverent praise to him must be at least equal to that which he felt and sought to express.

In acknowledging the divine greatness, the one who prays is also acknowledging his own position relative to God.

Recognize Your Blessings. The second letter of the word pray should prompt you to *recognize your blessings* as you speak to God in prayer.

Every good gift of a material nature we enjoy is from God (Jas. 1:17); all spiritual blessings are ours because of the redemption we have received through the blood of Christ (Eph. 1:3). As we pray, we need to be very specific in naming our blessings and acknowledging the love and generosity of God which sent them to us.

Even in times of loss and pain, when our purpose in prayer is to seek the aid of God, we should preface our requests with thanks and gratitude for the things he has done for us in the past.

Acknowledge Needs. The third letter of the word tells you to *acknowledge your needs to God* in prayer.

Paul reminded his readers that God is able to meet our every requirement through his power and love. "And my God shall supply every need of yours according to his riches in glory in Christ Jesus" (Phil. 4:19). In times of sickness, trouble, or sorrow, cast your burden on the Lord through prayer: "Let us therefore draw near with boldness unto the throne of grace, that we may receive mercy, and may find grace to help us in time of need" (Heb. 4:16).

When you need to be strong in the face of temptation, seek the Lord in prayer. This is the counsel of Paul at Ephesians 6:10-11, 18. When you need guidance in making difficult decisions in your life, pray about the matter. "In all thy ways acknowledge him and he will direct thy paths" (Prov. 3:6). When you sin, ask the forgiving God of heaven to pardon you. Pray as David did for the Lord to blot our your transgressions (Psa. 51:1-2), and rise from that prayer in the confidence that he has. God hears the prayers of his children.

Yearn for Others. The last letter of the word pray

suggests that you *express your yearnings for others* to the Father in heaven.

The point has been made already that selfishness has no place in effective and meaningful prayer. As you pray, then, think about others and their needs as well as your own. Pray for the lost (Rom. 10:1), and pray for your brothers and sisters who have sinned (Jas. 5:16). The Bible commands us to pray for the leaders of government (1 Tim. 2:1-2). We should pray for elders, preachers, and missionaries. The sick, aged, and poor need our prayers. It is even a good idea to keep a list of specific persons and situations which you want to pray about regularly.

When these four elements are included in your prayers, you can be sure that they are scriptural and acceptable to the God we worship.

Conclusion

This chapter has sought to emphasize the privilege and procedures of prayer. In order for these lessons to be learned, however, the student must actually begin to pray.

God is there and waiting to hear from you. He stands ready to respond to your requests. You cannot imagine what it will mean to your spiritual growth to be a person of regular prayer until you have tried it for a while.

Henry Ford once bought a million-dollar insurance policy on his life. A good friend of his, who was in the insurance business, asked why he had not bought the policy from him. The answer came back, "You didn't ask me to."

How many good things of God are we missing simply because we do not pray? "Ye have not, because ye ask not" (Jas. 4:2b).

SOME THINGS TO THINK ABOUT

1. There seems to be both a logical and practical reason for associating prayer with personal Bible study. Do you agree? What are some of the occasions of your life which have made you feel the need for prayer most keenly?

2. Several reasons are given in this chapter which justify viewing prayer as a *privilege*. Give some attention to each. What would you add to this list?

3. What are some of the things the Bible teaches us to ask for in our prayers? How is it a test of our faith to be told to pray for these things?

4. This chapter discusses several conditions of acceptable prayer. Study each closely. Be sure that you understand the practical implications of each.

5. What are some of the values of public prayers over private? Of private over public? What are some of the special distractions one must guard against in leading public prayers?

6. An acrostic on the word "pray" was offered as a means to guidance about how to engage in this spiritual exercise. Do you find it helpful?

7. What can you do to make prayer more important and more effective in your spiritual life?

Chapter Eight

Living Spiritually: The Church

The English word "church" is derived from the Greek adjective *kuriakos,* which means "belonging to the Lord." The word translated "church" in the New Testament is *ekklesia,* "a called-out body."

The church is the locus of the work of God's kingdom on earth, i.e., his reign in the hearts of men. This church began on Pentecost Day of A.D. 30, and it has survived through history whenever and wherever the gospel of Christ has been taught, believed, and obeyed.

Although it seems popular today to disparage the church, the Word of God gives it a central place in the scheme of redemption. The church is the body of Christ and the "fulness of him that filleth all in all" (Eph. 1:22-23). To say that it is the fulness (i.e., completion) of our Lord is to make a grand claim for it. It indicates that the church "completes" Christ in the sense that it is the means by which he functions in the world to save men. It is the visible manifestation of his ongoing work of salvation among humankind.

As we continue to study about spiritual living and Christian growth, we must devote some time to a study of the importance of the church. Such is the purpose of this chapter.

Why Jesus Established the Church

In spite of the general tendency to disparage the role of the local church, Christ had very specific purposes in view when he founded this body. Each of them ultimately looks to the spiritual needs of Christians. Notice three of his reasons for bringing the church into being as we begin this chapter.

Fellowship. First, the local church of Christ is intended to be *a center for fellowship and mutual encouragement among believers.* In the last book of the Old Testament, written around 400 B.C., God sought to call a slothful and spiritually lethargic people to penitence and anticipation of the Messiah. A result of Malachi's prophetic ministry was as follows: "Then they that feared Jehovah spake one with another; and Jehovah hearkened, and heard, and a book of remembrance was written before him, for them that feared Jehovah, and that thought upon his name" (Mal. 3:16). Notice the key acts of turning in these people as they began to fear the Lord. The shaking off of their past indifference was marked by (1) being together, (2) speaking with one another about God, and (3) thinking on his purposes for their lives.

The people of the Lord in every generation need the spiritual stimulation that comes of being together, speaking with one another about the God they love and serve, and meditating on his purposes for them.

We have certain social needs for friendship and community, and the fellowship of the church is designed to meet and satisfy them. We share sorrows and joys (Rom. 12:15), encourage one another in things that are good (Heb. 10:24), pick up the brother or sister who stumbles (Gal. 6:1), and rejoice over our mutual hope in Christ.

Worship. Second, the local church of God is *a society of worshippers*. God both deserves and desires worship from his human creatures (cf. John 4:24), and the church is that special group of redeemed people authorized to serve as a priesthood for the offering up of the worship he is due. We fail to see ourselves in true perspective if we neglect the worship of our Creator and Sustainer.

Each part of the church's worship meets a vital need in our spiritual lives. The teaching of the Word of God nurtures faith (Rom. 10:17), singing exhorts us to spiritual living and praises the deity we adore (Col. 3:16), giving of our money to finance the work of the church makes us partners in the work of God and keeps us from selfishness (2 Cor. 9:7), our united prayers give us power with God in the certain knowledge that he hears and will answer our requests (Jas. 5:16b), and the Lord's Supper is an event of spiritual renewal that takes us back to the time and place of the central episode in the whole redemption drama (1 Cor. 10:16-17).

It is precisely because worship meets urgent needs in our spiritual lives that Christians are taught never to forsake their assembling together for worship (Heb. 10:25).

Good Works. Third, the church is *a place of organized labor and service*. No loose association of people – no matter how devoted or determined – can become a significant movement. Such powerful movements as Communism, the Red Cross, or a dynamic local church depend on efficient organization for their success.

With elders as the overseers of their activities (Acts 20:28), local churches must be organized for the accomplishment of specific works in the service of God. The gospel must be taught to our own people and to outsiders, the poor and discouraged need help, and we must be ready unto every good work. These goals will be reached more effectively through organized programs than through hit-or-miss efforts.

IdentifyiNq MARks of Christ's ChuRch

As the church functions in harmony with the purposes for which the Lord established it, there are certain peculiar characteristics (i.e., identifying marks) which must remain in evidence. At whatever time any one of them is neglected by a body of people, that group runs the risk of losing its identity. What once was a church can wind up being nothing more than a club if it sacrifices these distinctive qualities.

We will examine the identifying traits of a faithful church under four headings: doctrinal soundness, holy living, discipline, and outreach.

Doctrinal Soundness. Faithfulness to the doctrinal content of the gospel is the foremost challenge to the church in every generation and at every location in the world. After all, even non-religious groups can be committed to high morality, could discipline members who are disloyal to those standards, and might have a policy of outreach to others. Why would such groups not be "churches"? There can be only one answer to this question: *they lack the doctrinal tenets and commitments of the church.*

We are the church of Christ because of what we believe and have done in our lives on the authority of the Word of God. We believe in the existence of the infinite, personal God of heaven and earth; we believe that he has revealed himself to us through prophets and apostles who were led by the Holy Spirit; we believe that he showed himself to us most uniquely in the person of Jesus of Nazareth. We accept certain doctrines about Jesus and his role in salvation – that he was born of a virgin, that he died on the cross to provide atonement for our sins, that he was raised bodily from the tomb, and that he rules over his people from heaven until such time as he shall appear to judge the world. An excellent summary of these doctrines is found at Philippians 2:5-11, and you should pause from your reading of this chapter to read these few verses carefully.

In terms of human responsibility in salvation, the Scripture teaches that an individual receives the remission of his sins and puts on Christ at the time of his baptism in Jesus' name (Acts. 2:38; Gal. 3:26-27). We cannot teach any other doctrine of salvation and still be faithful to the doctrinal content of the Word of God. The New Testament reveals a pattern of organization for local churches which must be respected. Elders oversee all the functions of the church (1 Pet. 5:2), deacons minister in responsibilities assigned by the elders (Acts 6:1-3), and every member of the congregation respects and submits to the leadership of the elders (Heb. 13:17).

In terms of worship, work projects, and other activities

of the church, the doctrinal correctness of the belief or practice in question must be of primary concern. We are God's faithful people only so long as we abide in the truth. "Whosoever goeth onward and abideth not in the teaching of Christ, hath not God: he that abideth in the teaching, the same hath both the Father and the Son" (2 John 9).

Holy Living. Not only must our beliefs and teachings be distinctive, but our manner of daily living must be equally distinctive. "Only let your manner of life be worthy of the gospel of Christ" (Phil. 1:27). "And be not fashioned according to this world: but be ye transformed by the renewing of your mind, that ye may prove what is the good and acceptable and perfect will of God" (Rom. 12:2).

In the first chapter of this book, the point was made that one's conversion marks a radical commitment of his life. It cannot be viewed merely as "turning over a new leaf" or giving up a few bad habits. Making Jesus Christ the Savior and Lord of your life obligates you to a standard of high and holy living which has no equal. Living the Christian life is demanding and difficult. It entails living with a sense of alienation from the world: "Love not the world, neither the things that are in the world. If any man love the world, the love of the Father is not in him" (1 John 2:15).

A Christian is truthful and honest. He keeps his speech pure of defilement. He does not allow himself to take up enslaving habits which destroy his influence for the Lord. His conscious purpose in everything he does is to glorify God (cf. 1 Cor. 10:31).

Discipline. A third mark of the church is internal self-discipline. When members of the local body of believers turn aside from the doctrine of Christ or repudiate the holy life they are called to live in favor of sinful behavior which is deliberate, the remainder of that group must take action for that person's sake.

First, it is the responsibility of the church to exhort, rebuke, teach, and bring back the erring brother. "Brethren, even if a man be overtaken in any trespass, ye who are spiritual, restore such a one in a spirit of gentleness; looking to thyself, lest thou also be tempted" (Gal. 6:1). If this effort fails, the entire church must withdraw its fellowship from the Christian who has gone back to the world. "Now we command you, brethren, in the name of our Lord Jesus Christ, that ye withdraw yourselves from every brother that walketh disorderly, and not after the tradition which they received from us" (2 Thess. 3:6). The purpose of this punitive action is not to crush and damn the person in his apostasy; it is to shame and sober him so he will repent and be saved (1 Cor. 5:5).

Even the Lions Club disciplines its members. The person who repudiates the club, attends no more of its meetings, and works against its goals is not going to be perpetually recognized as a member of that social organization. But churches seem to be reluctant to take this step against their wayward members. This hesitation both involves the church in sin (for not obeying the New Testament) and does a disservice to the erring brother or sister. "My brethren, if any among you err from the truth, and one convert him; let him know that he who converteth a sinner from the error of his way shall save a soul from death, and shall cover a multitude of sins" (Jas. 5:19-20).

Outreach. The final trait of a faithful church we shall look at is evangelistic outreach. The church exists in this world as an extension of Christ himself – it is his spiritual body – for the seeking and saving of lost men. We do not exist just for our own sakes (i.e., worship, instruction, etc.) but for the sake of people who do not know our Savior. It is our responsibility to share the knowledge of Christ with the world.

Separation from the world does not require *isolation* from it. Jesus is our perfect example here. He was separate from the world's attitudes, sinful behavior, and God-defying lifestyle. Yet he went among worldly people – talked with them, ate with them, opened his heart to them – for the sake of ministering to their needs and calling them to the Father of our spirits.

The early church was a community of evangelists. Each believer appears to have seen himself or herself as a *missionary*. That this is true can be seen from many events in the book of Acts. For example, when Christians in and around Jerusalem were scattered by a great persecution at the hands of the Jews, they took their message to their new locations and planted the kingdom of God in additional places throughout Palestine. "They therefore that were scattered abroad went about preaching the word" (Acts 8:4).

There are still places in our world where the gospel is not being heard and where the church does not exist. Yet Christians go to these towns and counties and countries as salesmen, teachers, government workers, and businessmen. Why do we not take the gospel with us? Have we consigned evangelism to the "professionals" (i.e., preachers, missionaries, etc.) and forgotten that it is the business of the whole body of Christ?

The Role You Fill

This leads us to the logical question at this point about the role believers fill in the church. Where do you fit as a member of the body of Christ?

First, see yourself as *a vital part of the local church*. Don't speak of "them" and "their" plans or work. Always talk about "us" and "our" projects for the Lord. Realize that the church is the one organization in all the world where every single member really does count. For each Christian who is not actively involved in the work of the church, there is some work of God in this world which is being left undone.

Paul's analogy of the church in 1 Corinthians 12 is the familiar one of a human body. "For as the body is one, and hath many members, and all the members of the body, being many, are one body; so also is Christ" (v. 12). Perhaps the most important point to be made from his analogy is this: *"For the body is not one member, but many"* (v. 14). Just as the physical body is handicapped and malfunctioning when any part of it is not doing its job, so also is the body of Christ handicapped if you are not providing your function.

Second, *be regular in your presence for and participation in its public services.* Any organized group has the right to expect its members to show their loyalty to it with their presence and participation in its meetings. This is a minimal expectation, but some see it as too high a price to pay in their spiritual lives in Christ. What a shallow view of spirituality these people are displaying.

The Bible has a great deal to say about the sin of neglect. For example, "To him therefore that knoweth to do good,

111

and doeth it not, to him it is sin" (James 4:17). Would anyone deny that it is doing "good" to be present for the worship of God? How, then, can we think it is an inconsequential matter to forsake the assemblies of the church?

Third, *be a cheerful, generous, and regular giver.* "But this I say, He that soweth sparingly shall reap also sparingly; and he that soweth bountifully shall reap also bountifully. Let each man do according as he hath purposed in his heart: not grudgingly, or of necessity: for God loveth a cheerful giver" (2 Cor. 9:6-7).

One's cancelled checks tell a great deal about that individual's character and interests. The woman who writes a number of checks to antique shops and furniture stores is doing something for her house. The man who writes checks to the boat shop and fishing tackle store is getting ready to go after fish. The man or woman who regularly writes checks to the church and to good works tells of his or her concern for the work of God in this world.

Fourth, let people see you as *a worthy representative of the purity and righteousness for which the church stands.* Jesus Christ has given us his name to wear, and our lives are reflecting either honor or dishonor to him. A young person's behavior at school, a wife's diligence in meeting the needs of her family, and a man's integrity in his work – all these are noticed by the world as a reflection of that Christian's commitment to the Lord. All of us know of individuals who have been led to salvation by the good example of some believer. We also know of people who have nothing but contempt for the church because some Christian cheated him in a business deal or otherwise failed to live by the standard of righteousness to which he is committed as a member of the body of Christ.

There are some works of the church which you may be unable to participate in because of a lack of ability or training in that area. But one thing *every* Christian can do is to be mindful of his or her influence. We must "give no occasion of stumbling" to those people whose lives we contact (cf. 1 Cor. 10:32-33).

Fifth, *use your special abilities and training in the work of the church*. If you have the ability to teach school or to train workers in a plant or sales corporation, you can also learn and teach the Bible to others. If you have an outgoing personality or prominence in some field of achievement, use the influence you have gained thereby to lead those who like you or admire your success to show them the path to eternal life. If you have administrative or leadership ability with your company, you can use those same abilities for helping organize and direct activities of the church under the oversight.

It has always bothered me that multi-talented folk in business, professions, and community service are sometimes reluctant to assume any responsibility for using those same skills to some spiritual advantage. Can God be pleased if we use the abilities he has given us selfishly? Or did he give them to us for the sake of enabling us to glorify him?

Perhaps your response to this point is to say that you have nothing "special" to use in service to the Lord. Maybe you are not a leader in your city or prominent in some field. In fact, it could be the case that you learned of Christ while in prison. Or perhaps your life has been one of tragedy and illness rather than fame and accomplishment. Maybe you are divorced. These circumstances do not make you unable to mediate the grace of God to people. They may give you special compassion for such work. Others may listen to you simply because they know you have been where they are – and have overcome by the power of Christ. Every Christian has some special ability which can be used to advantage in the work of the Lord.

Sixth, *love your brothers and sisters.* Negatively, don't take offense and assume the worst about every statement or action of your brothers and sisters in Christ. Don't run your tongue to say unkind (even if true) things about them. Don't create friction in the church by allowing any sort of unresolved grievance between you and someone else. "But if ye bite and devour one another, take heed that ye be not consumed one of another" (Gal. 5:15). Positively, be alert to the needs of your brothers and sisters, and willingly give of yourself to serve those needs. "Not looking each of you to his own things, but each of you also to the things of others" (Phil. 2:4).

Love for one another is supposed to be a special characteristic of the disciples of Christ. "A new commandment I give unto you, that ye love one another; even as I have loved you, that ye also love one another. By this shall all men know that ye are my disciples, if ye have love one to another" (John 13:34-35).

Conclusion

It is by design of God that every saved person is identified with a group of believers, i.e., the church. God knows that we cannot develop into the spiritual people he wants us to be in isolation from others who are moving toward the same goal. So, no matter what excuses or rationalizations one may bring forth, he can never justify bypassing the church.

Love Christ's church and supply your function for its well-being as the body of Christ. It is an essential part of your attempt to go on to maturity.

Some Things To Think About

1. The word *church* is generally used today to refer to a denomination as opposed to the body of Christ revealed in Scripture. Give some thought to how important it is for us to keep the New Testament concept of the church fixed in our minds.

2. Three reasons for the establishment of the church are given at the beginning of the chapter. Reflect on each one. What other reason(s) for its establishment can you suggest?

3. What does "doctrinal soundness" signify? Does a commitment to doctrinal purity justify suspicion and "witch hunts" among brethren? Must one be unloving in character in order to insist on doctrinal soundness?

4. Will the world listen to the truth of God's Word if it is spoken by people whose lives are impure? Examine several Bible passages other than the ones cited in this chapter which exhort God's people to holy living. What is the practical basis for these appeals?

5. Are local churches obligated to internal self-discipline by the New Testament? How faithful do we tend to be in this regard? How can failure on this point be defended at the Judgment?

6. Can evangelism be left to a group of paid "professionals" in the church? How can such a tendency be resisted?

7. What are the personal responsibilities which every Christian must assume in order to fill his or her proper place in the church of God?

Chapter Nine

A Checklist
On Attitudes

You have almost certainly noticed that different people react to the same situations in radically different ways. At the death of a close loved one, for example, some people withdraw, become bitter, and denounce God. In other cases of equally great bereavement, the parties involved bear their loss with grace and draw closer to the Lord through it. The same sort of observations could be made about times of serious illness, family problems, financial reverses, etc.

Neither could you have failed to notice how different certain relationships are with some people as opposed to others. In some marriages, the husband and wife are obviously committed to each other in genuine love and enjoy their life together. In others, a man and woman stay at each other's throats constantly and make themselves and everyone around them miserable. Some churches are made up of godly people who are positive and helpful toward every good work. Others have the appearance of a group of disgruntled misfits who see their work as finding fault and criticizing.

Could the differences described above be accounted for by something so elemental as one's *attitudes* toward the people, things, and events around him or her?

Scientists have frequently observed the close relationship of mind to body. Embarrassment causes one to blush; exhaustion makes a man irritable; a sense of being loved causes a woman to feel contented and warm. The Bible records many examples of people whose attitudes led them to certain ends. The positive attitude of Job caused him to trust the Almighty through an incredible series of catastrophes; the negative spirit of Judas made him complain about the loving acts of others toward Jesus and, ultimately, to betray our Lord for thirty pieces of silver.

Your success or failure in living the Christian life depends largely on the attitudes you foster in living it. In this chapter, we shall look for some basic attitudes which are commended to Christians in the Bible. These are traits of spirit which will bless you and everyone around you.

Although others could surely be added to this checklist, there are seven qualities identified here which are invaluable for going on to maturity.

Optimism

There are many Bible passages which encourage the people of God to maintain an optimistic spirit amid life's fluctuating fortunes. Solomon taught that good things will come to the person who embraces the promises of God and puts his trust in him. "He that giveth heed unto the word shall find good; and whoso trusteth in Jehovah, happy is he" (Prov. 16:20). Paul taught the saints at Rome to rejoice in this confidence: "What then shall we say to these things? If God is for us, who is against us?" (Rom. 8:31). When he wrote to the church at Philippi, the same apostle told his readers to rejoice in the peace and strength of Jesus. "Rejoice in the Lord always: again I will say, Rejoice. Let your forbearance be known unto all men. The Lord is at hand. In nothing be anxious; but in everything by prayer and supplication with thanksgiving let your requests be made known unto God. And the peace of God, which passeth all understanding, shall guard your hearts and your thoughts in Christ Jesus. ... I can do all things in him that strengtheneth me" (Phil. 4:4-7, 13).

Optimism gives one a sense of confidence and courage in living the Christian life. Some Christians seem defeated from the start: Can I be faithful? Can I hold out to the end? I can never do any great work for the Lord! As surely as one dwells on the likelihood of failure, he will fail. Trust in the Lord for daily strength in your task, and you will succeed.

One word of caution should be sounded here. Don't confuse Christian optimism with believing in self. The Christian's confidence arises from the fact that he believes in God. His optimism is grounded in *God-confidence rather than self-confidence.*

GENEROSITY

Selfishness is one of the ugliest of attitudes; generosity is one of the most beautiful. Paul had experience in trying

119

to work with some in his day who were of the former disposition. He lamented, "For they all seek their own, not the things of Jesus Christ" (Phil. 2:21).

Selfishness causes some people to seek their own pleasure in opposition to the things of Christ. Examples of this sort of person would range from the silversmiths of ancient Ephesus (Acts 19:27-29) to the modern drug pushers and porno peddlers. Such individuals do not care about righteousness and feel no compassion for the people they are hurting.

Selfishness causes some to seek their own interests to the degree that they simply neglect the things of Christ. These people are not so blatantly wicked as the drug pusher, for their concerns are legitimate and moral. Their fault is in getting so wrapped up in them that they have no time for the Lord. In one of his parables, Jesus told of people who were bidden to a marriage feast. "But they made light of it, and went their ways, one to his own farm, another to his merchandise" (Matt. 22:5). Applying his parable to modern situations, these people represent men who are so busy with their businesses that they cannot attend the services of the church or women who are so caught up in civic work that they have no time to work for the Lord's church.

The same selfish spirit manifests itself occasionally even among those who are active in doing things for Christ and his church. It shows its ugly head by causing people to put too much of themselves into what they do for the Lord. What sorts of persons are these? They are like the Pharisees who did their good works "that they may be seen of men" (Matt. 23:5-7). These are people who try to use the work of Christ to make a name for themselves (cf.

Phil. 1:15). They are folk who love the spotlight but who will not do behind-the-scenes work.

While it is right to concentrate on school, business, civic, and other duties, it is wrong to be so wholly taken up with self in these pursuits that one cannot see outside his own little world. That is the essence of being a selfish person.

By contrast, a generous spirit will manifest itself in a sincere interest in other people. This type person looks not only to his own interests but also tries to find ways to encourage and help others (cf. Phil. 2:4). He demonstrates a willingness to extend himself for the other person's welfare (cf. 1 Cor. 9:19-23).

A biblical appeal for children of God to nurture the spirit of generosity is found in these words: "Put on therefore, as God's elect, holy and beloved, a heart of compassion, kindness, lowliness, meekness, longsuffering; forbearing one another, and forgiving each other, if any man have a complaint against any; even as the Lord forgave you, so also do ye: and above all these things put on love, which is the bond of perfectness" (Col. 3:12-14).

Tolerance

Another attitude which helps make for success in Christian living is tolerance. Toward false beliefs and sinful actions which would compromise the doctrine of Christ, the faithful child of God must demonstrate absolute intolerance (cf. Gal. 2:4-5; 2 John 9-11). In the routine relationships of his life, however, he should try to show the broadest degree of tolerance toward other people and their actions.

Human beings are not all alike. We have different personalities, tastes, cultural backgrounds, etc. It makes for better living when one is able to recognize, accept, and live with the differences he sees in the people around him. It usually helps one to be more tolerant of others when he stops to think how tolerant those people are having to be withhis peculiarities!

"So then let us follow after things which make for peace, and things whereby we may edify one another" (Rom. 14:19). Among other things, this verse implies that the inability to be patient with the peculiarities, weaknesses, and failures of others is an unhealthy thing. The Lord does not want his people sitting in judgment on one another about such trivial matters. In the Sermon on the Mount, he said, "Judge not, that ye be not judged. For with what judgment ye judge, ye shall be judged: and with what measure ye mete, it shall be measured unto you. And why beholdest thou the mote that is in thy brother's eye, but considerest not the beam that is in thine own eye?" (Matt. 7:1-3). If each of us would devote himself to self-criticizing and self-improvement with the same degree of passion we put into criticizing and nagging others, the result would be far more beneficial.

In too many places where tolerance is found, it serves a wrong cause (e.g., countenancing a false teacher); in the places where it could render real service to the Lord's work (e.g., keeping peace among brethren), it often is lacking. Remember that this spirit does not arise because one "could care less" about the issue at stake but in spite of one's own strong opinion or preference. Tolerance does not grow out of indifference but love.

Humility

The Bible enjoins the spirit of humility in several different settings. Of course, children of God must be humble before our Father in heaven. "For thus saith the high and lofty One that inhabiteth eternity, whose name is Holy: I dwell in the high and holy place, and with him also that is of a contrite and humble spirit, to revive the spirit of the humble, and to revive the heart of the contrite" (Isa. 57:15; cf. Jas. 4:6; Luke 18:13). Christians are also to be humble among ourselves: "Do nothing from selfishness or conceit, but in humility count others better than yourselves" (Phil. 2:3 RSV). With whatever service we render in the kingdom of God, the glory which might come of it is to be given to the Lord rather than held for oneself (cf. Matt. 5:16).

Just what is humility? It is not some sort of external mortification of the body (Matt. 6:16). It is not a doleful face, gloomy temperament, or bent posture (Matt. 6:17). Neither is it a false humility which protests that one is simply unworthy to come to God, partake of the Lord's Supper, accept a position of service in the church, etc.

Humility is the opposite of pride and self-exaltation. It is the virtue Jesus commended to us when he said, "Blessed are the poor in spirit: for theirs is the kingdom of heaven" (Matt. 5:3). It is the attitude Paul displayed when he wrote: "But far be it from me to glory, save in the cross of our Lord Jesus Christ, through which the world hath been crucified unto me, and I unto the world" (Gal. 6:14). Humility is a recognition of our dependence on the grace of God (cf. 1 Tim. 1:15) and an acceptance of our proper position relative to other men before God (cf. Rom. 12:3).

A helpful parable related to this point is found in the Gospel of Luke. "Suppose one of you had a servant plowing or looking after the sheep. Would he say to the servant when he comes in from the field, 'Come along now and sit down to eat?' Would he not rather say, 'Prepare my supper, get yourself ready and wait on me while I eat and drink; after that you may eat and drink'? Would he thank the servant because he did what he was told to do? So you also, when you have done everything you were told to do, should say, 'We are unworthy servants; we have only done our duty'" (Luke 17:7-10 NIV). As servants of God, it is our responsibility to toil and labor in the kingdom. We must not expect praise for each thing we do; we simply serve. We do things which are our duty to do. It is humility which prompts this sort of service for the Lord.

Gratitude

One of the most charming things about children is their ability to show joy over and gratitude for the things they receive. One of the most annoying things about most of us as we grow up is that we lose that ability and come to expect even more than we receive, act very indifferently toward what we receive, and show very little gratitude.

We are all dependent creatures before the Lord. From his bounteous hand, we receive life, health, joy of family and friends, spiritual blessings in Christ, etc. Beyond these, most of us have received certain special blessings for which we are particularly indebted to him.

Do we give God the praise and thanksgiving he deserves? Do we let others know how gracious he is by attributing our blessings to him in their presence? Do we serve him with the devotion his generosity merits? "Oh that men would praise Jehovah for his lovingkindness, and for his wonderful works to the children of men" (Psa. 107:8).

COMPASSION

Compassion is a sympathetic awareness of the needs of others and a sincere desire to minister to those needs. This spirit seems to be disappearing from the populace in general. We have become cynical toward people in distress and aloof from our fellow men. In July of 1983, dozens of adults watched two boys rape a 13-year-old girl in a public park in St. Louis. Only one person acted to do anything for her – an 11-year-old boy named Sur Williams. He pedaled down the street on his bicycle, brought the police, and helped identify the attackers. We ask ourselves how this sort of thing can happen!

Even Christians have sometimes given way to the cynicism and aloofness of our day. We sometimes adopt a what's-the-use attitude which excuses us from doing anything on behalf of the poor, the hungry, the downcast, and the lost.

Jesus is our perfect example of tender compassion toward others. "And Jesus went about all the cities and the villages, teaching in their synagogues, and preaching the gospel of the kingdom, and healing all manner of disease and all manner of sickness. But when he saw the multitudes, he was moved with compassion for them, because they were distressed and scattered, as sheep not having a shepherd" (Matt. 9:35-36).

We are supposed to imitate his example in all things. In our attitude toward the sick, suffering, and needy, we need

125

to be tender and helpful. With regard to men and women who are lost in sin, we need to show compassion rather than self-righteousness. When our brothers and sisters have problems and needs, our hearts must reach out to them.

Faithfulness

Finally, the child of God needs to develop a general life pattern of faithfulness in all his deeds. The Savior taught: "He that is faithful in a very little is faithful also in much: and he that is unrighteous in a very little is unrighteous in much" (Luke 16:10). The individual who wants the great task in the kingdom of God without faithfully executing the small ones he has been given does not deserve to have his wish granted.

From our experiences with people, we know that the hard-working person at his job, farming, housework, or schoolwork is the same person who can be relied on to be active in the work of the church. Such people have developed a general pattern of response of life's duties and opportunities which carries over into everything else. So take every responsibility seriously. Your faithfulness – or the lack of it – shows up in diligence in your studies, performance on your job, attending worship services, etc. Each of these is a test of your worthiness to be entrusted with some greater responsibility.

Looking back over your spiritual life, are you more faithful in the things of Christ today than a year ago? Paul lamented that some Christians of his acquaintance were decreasing in their dependability. He told them, "Ye were running well; who hindered you that ye should not obey the truth?" (Gal. 5:7). On the analogy of running a race, the person who drops out before crossing the finish line has no hope of winning. Your salvation depends on the development of stedfastness in your faith and life.

Conclusion

Attitudes really do determine actions. The state of mind we bring to the situation often makes the difference in having it turn out well or fail. It is the same with Christian growth and maturity.

Use the little checklist given in this chapter to take inventory of your heart. Are your attitudes positive and strong enough to see you through to spiritual maturity in Christ?

Some Things To Think About

1. What is optimism? What traits distinguish the person with an optimistic outlook on life? Distinguish self-confidence from God-confidence.

2. What actions typify a person who is generous in spirit? What actions characterize the person with an opposite disposition? In your opinion, what Bible character (other than Jesus) best exemplifies generosity?

3. In what situations must Christians be intolerant and inflexible? Tolerant and willing to yield? What harm is produced when we confuse these situations?

4. Cite several Bible texts which enjoin humility upon the people of God. Does the parable of Luke 17:7-10 help you understand the type of humility required of Christians?

5. Locate a biblical character and/or episode which helps impress the need of gratitude on your mind. What are some of the special blessings of your life for which

you are especially grateful? How do you express your feelings?

6. Define compassion. Do you agree that this spirit is becoming rare in contemporary settings? What can Christians do to guard our hearts from callousness and indifference?

7. How are the routine things of life suitable to judge one's faithfulness? Is this fair? What are the implications of Luke 16:10 for one's usefulness in the work of the church?

Chapter Ten

Obedience

Among all the "four-letter words" in the English language, this one seems to be particularly offensive: O-B-E-Y.

There is something of the maverick within each of us that tends to resist authority and disregard rules. The balking child at naptime, an impatient adult behind the wheel of an automobile, and many religious people in the face of Bible commandments —all have something in common.

The problem is not new to our age. Men have always resisted God and the demands of his holy will on their sinful lives. During his earthly ministry, Jesus lamented, "And why call ye me, Lord, Lord, and do not the things which I say?" (Luke 6:46). Therefore the general appeal of the Scripture is this: "Do not merely listen to the word, and so deceive yourselves. Do what it says" (James 1:22 NIV).

A Gallup Poll of a few years ago said U.S. citizens are "impressively religious" on the surface. The same poll revealed, however, that three out of four of the persons surveyed "do not connect religion with their judgments of right and wrong."

Some religious groups foster this attitude with their false doctrine of "once saved always saved." If a man is going to heaven unconditionally, why should he bother with conscientious obedience to commands? The abhorrent nature of such a doctrine was brought home to a father whose teen-aged son was making light of his deliberate disobedience. "Don't worry, Dad," he said, "I'm saved, and I'll go to heaven when I die!"

At the risk of being called "legalists," we must emphasize the necessary place of obedience in one's spiritual life as he goes on to maturity.

Contrasting Attitudes Toward Divine Commands

In the Old Testament, there are two contrasting examples of men and their attitudes toward the authority of God. The former case involves King Saul, and the latter one relates the story of Daniel and his three friends in Babylon.

The Almighty God of Israel gave this command to Saul: "Now go and smite Amalek, and utterly destroy all that they have, and spare them not; but slay both man and woman, infant and suckling, ox and sheep, camel and ass" (1 Sam. 15:3). The armies of Israel were to be used of God on this campaign to execute a whole nation of idolatrous people; their whole civilization was to be annihilated from the face of the earth. How faithful was Saul to his responsibility as a minister of divine wrath? "But

Saul and the people spared Agag, and the best of the sheep, and of the oxen, and the fatlings, and the lambs, and all that was good, and would not utterly destroy them: but everything that was vile and refuse, that they destroyed utterly" (1 Sam. 15:9). Notice how *selective* their "obedience" was. They utterly destroyed what they regarded as worthless and spared what they felt to be useful – in spite of God's clear charge that nothing was to remain of these people or their depraved culture.

When Saul and his armies returned home from this campaign, the prophet Samuel was sent by the Lord to challenge the king for his actions. Samuel said, "Though thou wast little in thine own sight, wast thou not made the head of the tribes of Israel? And Jehovah anointed thee king over Israel; and Jehovah sent thee on a journey, and said, Go, and utterly destroy the sinners the Amalekites, and fight against them until they be consumed. *Wherefore then didst thou not obey the voice of Jehovah,* but didst fly upon the spoil, and didst that which was evil in the sight of Jehovah?" (1 Sam. 15:17-19).

Saul's reply was pathetically weak. First, he remonstrated with Samuel and said, "Yea, I have obeyed the voice of Jehovah." Then, admitting in his own account of the events which had transpired that he had not done all the Lord sent him to do, he next tried to shift the full blame from his shoulders by placing the responsibility for what had happened on the armies. "But the people took of the spoil, sheep and oxen, the chief of the devoted things, to sacrifice unto Jehovah thy God in Gilgal" (1 Sam. 15:20-21).

None of these defenses was allowed to stand. The final disposition of the matter involved rebuke and rejection for the once-mighty King Saul. "And Samuel said, Hath Jehovah as great delight in burnt-offerings and sacrifices, as in obeying the voice of Jehovah? Behold, to obey is better than sacrifice, and to hearken than the fat of rams. For rebellion is as the sin of witchcraft, and stubbornness is as idolatry and teraphim. *Because thou hast rejected the word of Jehovah, he hath also rejected thee from being king"* (1 Sam. 15:22-23). What a sad and dismal end to a career so nobly begun by a once-humble and submissive Saul.

Quite the opposite of Saul, however, was the character Daniel. Carried away from his homeland to Babylon by Nebuchadnezzar in 606 B.C., he and his three friends – Shadrach, Meshach, and Abednego – were subjected to specially trying situations which tested their loyalty to God.

Selected by the Babylonians for special training which would allow them to serve in the government, these men were to be taught not only certain jobs but also the lifestyle of these pagans (Dan. 1:3-5). The special issues which came to be points of controversy were three. First, they were expected to eat certain foods which were unclean to the Jews and to drink the wine of the king (Dan. 1:8,11-12). Second, they were required to bow to and worship a golden image which Nebuchadnezzar erected (Dan. 3:1-7). Third, after the Babylonian kingdom fell to the Persians, conspiring satraps of that government secured the enactment of a law which made it a crime to pray to the God of Israel. The single purpose of this law was to secure the displacement of Daniel, a Jew who was resented for his prominence in the new government (Dan. 6:1-9).

What do you think *you* would have done under those circumstances? You are a prisoner in a foreign land; your God is unknown; and the best hope you have for surviving against very high odds is to cooperate with the conquering government. Perhaps you find it hard to find a quick rationalization for worshipping an idol, but what about the food and prayer? Might you be tempted to eat some of the unclean meat or to drink the king's wine? After all, it seems such a little thing. Couldn't you just miss praying for a few days? God would surely understand your omission under the circumstances.

While this sort of approach might be appealing to some of us, Daniel and his friends would have no part of any compromise. They stuck by the demands of their faith and were ready to take the consequences.

Take the consequences they did! Shadrach, Meshach, and Abednego were thrown into a fiery furnace for refusing to bow to the golden image (Dan. 3:20ff). Daniel was cast into a den of lions because of his persistence in prayer to the God of Israel (Dan. 6:16ff). God protected them miraculously and brought them through their ordeal without harm. *But even if they had died for their loyalty to the Lord – as many others have – their decision was the right one!* Their determination to obey the God of heaven resulted in obedience at great peril. It also resulted in their approval and vindication by the God they followed.

Now think seriously about these two episodes for a moment. Didn't Saul *almost* do all he was commanded to do? Didn't he destroy perhaps 95% of the Amalekites and their possessions? After all, wasn't the original demand a bit harsh? In the case of Daniel, might he not have been a bit legalistic? Does anyone really think God would have cast him off for eating a little flesh which would not have been considered kosher back in Palestine?

The very fact that questions of this sort can be raised seriously by people who study these accounts shows how far we have drifted from God! There is no way to defend Saul in his rebellion. There is nothing but praise due for Daniel and his friends for their actions.

Jesus and Obedience

In the *teaching* of Jesus, obedience is a frequent theme. To men still living under the Law of Moses, he said this about their obligation to that covenant: "Whosoever therefore shall break one of these least commandments, and shall teach men so, shall be called least in the kingdom of heaven: but whosoever shall do and teach them, he shall be called great in the kingdom of heaven" (Matt. 5:19). To those who desired to follow him, he said, "Not every one that saith unto me, Lord, Lord, shall enter into the kingdom of heaven; but he that doeth the will of my Father who is in heaven" (Matt. 7:21).

Our Lord said that his "family" consists of those who will be obedient to the Father in heaven. "For whosoever shall do the will of my Father who is in heaven, he is my brother, and sister, and mother" (Matt. 12:50). Perhaps more pointedly still, he said, "If ye love me, ye will keep my commandments. ... He that hath my commandments, and keepeth them, he it is that loveth me" (John 14:15,21a). To this he added that one's access to saving divine love is through obedience. "If ye keep my commandments, ye shall abide in my love; even as I have kept my Father's commandments, and abide in his love" (John 15:10).

Obedience was the theme of Jesus' *life* as well as his teaching. "Although he was a son, he learned obedience from what he suffered and, once made perfect, he became the source of eternal salvation for all who obey him" (Heb. 5:8-9 NIV).

It would be foolish for any one of us to call himself a follower of Jesus while minimizing obedience. To others it may be an oppressive burden, but for Christians the duty of obedience is a gentle yoke imposed by love.

The Relationship of Faith and Obedience

The Bible teaches that salvation is by grace through faith and is not capable of being earned through our works of merit (Eph. 2:8-9). Yet it also teaches that faith is real only when it demonstrates itself in obedience. Salvation is by grace, but it is not by force. By the love demonstrated on the cross, heaven woos us. Beyond that, nothing will be done to cause us to accept grace against our wills in the matter. Each of us is free to accept or reject it. The New Testament knows nothing of "irresistible grace."

Acceptance of divine grace is by faith; rejection comes about through unbelief. There is no acceptable obedience apart from faith; there is no acceptable faith apart from obedience.

Faith must be turned into deeds. Profession must issue in practice. "What good is it, my brothers, if a man claims to have faith but has no deeds? Can such faith save him? ... Show me your faith without deeds, and I will show you my faith by what I do ... As the body without the spirit is dead, so faith without deeds is dead" (James 2:14, 18b, 26 NIV).

Abraham is known to students of Scripture as the "father

of the faithful." How so? "By faith Abraham, when he was called, obeyed to go out unto a place which he was to receive for an inheritance. ... By faith Abraham, being tried, offered up Isaac" (Heb. 11:8,17). Abraham's faith and obedience are so intermingled that one cannot really say where the one ends and the other begins. Faith and obedience are always found in this inseparable relationship.

Obedience is simply faith in action. A faith which is professed is *mere profession* until it has been confirmed by submission to the will of God in actual obedience. The confession of the lips must be validated by the submission of the once-rebellious will.

This type of obedience is hardly legalism. Faith is one side of the coin, and deeds of obedience are the other; neither can exist apart from the other. *Faith without obedience is disobedience, and disobedience is nothing more nor less than blatant unbelief.*

The Obedience God Wants

Complete. The obedience which God desires of us is *complete obedience.* This is not to advocate "perfectionism" or the ability of a human being to render sinless obedience to all divine commands. Instead, it is to say that it is not our option to decide which of God's commands to obey. When God speaks, our only proper response is willing compliance with his expressed will.

Suppose a man has blueprints drawn for the house he wants built and delivers them to the builder. The builder sees that the plan calls for a bedroom on the northeast corner. "Good," he says, "for that arrangement allows its windows to catch the morning sunlight perfectly." The garage is to be on the southwest corner. "Fine," he says, "for that is the logical place for it in relation to the road-way already present." When he sees that the plan calls for a den on the southeast corner, he says, "Oh, this is all wrong! It would be much better to put the den near the garage and away from the bedroom, so I am going to build it on the the northwest corner." Question: *How many times did the builder submit to the demands of the blueprints?* Two of three times? The correct answer is *none.* In every single case, *he did as he wanted to do.* Two of the three times, his judgment happened to coincide with the plans given him! This is the type of rebellion God witnesses among his creatures so frequently. We do what he tells us to do – so long as we see the sense of it and agree it ought to be done. Yet we feel free to presume on him and change the plan when we see fit. Remember King Saul?

How beautiful is this commendation of a godly couple: "And they were both righteous before God, walking in all the commandments and ordinances of the Lord blame-less" (Luke 1:6). Surely it was their complete surrender to the divine will that allowed Zacharias and Elizabeth to be selected to bring the forerunner of the Messiah into the world through their home.

Cheerful. God also desires and has the right to expect our *cheerful obedience* to his will. Imagine the difference in a sullen child's grudging obedience and the eager obe-dience of mature love. Which does the Father in heaven want from his children?

For example, God has required gifts and offerings from his worshippers in every age of Bible history. It is not hard to imagine that some of these have been offered reluc-tantly. The intended good for the giver is denied him by virtue of the fact that he brings his offering in the wrong spirit. Paul wrote: "If I bestow all my goods to feed the poor ... but have not love, it profiteth me nothing" (1 Cor. 13:3). On this same topic of giving to the Lord, he later said, "Let each man do according as he hath purposed in his heart; not grudgingly, or of necessity: for God loveth a cheerful giver" (2 Cor. 9:7). Yes, God wants our gifts and offerings, but he wants them offered with a willing disposition.

The same observation can be made about any act of obedience to the Lord. He wants us to do what he has commanded, and he wants the deed performed willingly and cheerfully. Otherwise the obedience is marred.

Constant. It should also be pointed out that heaven wants our *constant obedience.* As the Christians of Galatia were reminded, a runner has not won the race until he crosses the finish line (Gal. 5:7). A good start in one's spiritual life can be in vain. Unless our complete and cheerful obedience is carried through to the end of our pilgrimage, we forfeit our security in Christ.

The point which has been made from the first page of this book is that God expects us to *grow* in spiritual things. Our knowledge must grow; our faith must grow; our love must grow. So must our obedience. Each day of one's life as a child of God should bring about a fuller surrender of that individual to the will of the Savior.

Conclusion

When Helen Keller was six years old, Miss Anne Sullivan came to teach this blind, deaf, and speechless child. Later she told a friend, "I saw clearly that it was useless to try to teach her language or anything else until she learned to obey me. I have thought about it a great deal, and the more I think the more certain I am that obedience is the gateway through which knowledge, yes, and love, too, enter the mind of a child" (Helen Keller, *The Story of My Life*, p. 265).

Miss Sullivan's observation about children is surely true of humanity generally. God has constantly stressed obedience that we might come to know his love in the truest and fullest sense. Therefore let it be our goal as maturing Christians to be daily "bringing every thought into captivity to the obedience of Christ" (2 Cor. 10:5).

Some Things To Think About

1. Other than religion, specify a number of other spheres of responsibility where obedience to authority is absolutely essential. Is there a general tendency toward rebellion against authority in all these areas, or is religion an exception?

2. Review the examples of Saul and Daniel. Show how Daniel could have rationalized in his circumstances so as to excuse disobedience.

3. What did Jesus have to say about obedience? What sort of example did he set? Study Hebrews 5:8-9 closely.

4. Is there a conflict between the biblical doctrines of faith and obedience? React to this statement from the chapter: "Faith without obedience is disobedience, and disobedience is nothing more nor less than blatant unbelief."

5. Read John 3:36 in both the King James and Revised Standard Versions. Do some research to find out why the translation varies. Which is correct? What is the implication of the more precise rendering?

6. This chapter suggests that God desires our complete,

cheerful, and constant obedience. What significance do you attach to each of these words?

7. React to Anne Sullivan's statement about obedience. Do you agree or disagree? What experiences from your own life support your answer?

Chapter Eleven

Tying Up
The Loose Ends

The conscientious Christian who is striving to grow in the grace and knowledge of Jesus Christ sometimes feels a sense of frustration in his efforts. So many things make demands on our time and attention. How shall we determine priorities? How can we "redeem the time" in these evil days? Our time is limited at best. So how do we discipline ourselves and manage our time to the best possible advantage?

Our Lord himself lived with a consciousness of the need to use time wisely and to the best advantage. He told his disciples, "We must work the works of him that sent me, while it is day: the night cometh, when no man can work" (John 9:4). This statement reflects the same sense of urgency about the right use of time that many of us struggle with today. The apostle Paul used the illustration of an athlete's self-discipline to describe his feelings about this matter. "And every man that striveth in the games exerciseth self-control in all things. Now they do it to receive a corruptible crown; but we an incorruptible. I therefore so run, as not uncertainly; so fight I, as not beating the air" (1 Cor. 9:25-26).

There is also the crucial matter of decision making. We want our lives to reflect maximum glory to God. Can we draw on the Lord's help in making decisions about career, marriage, and other personal concerns? The Bible makes this promise to children of God: "But if any of you lacketh wisdom, let him ask of God, who giveth to all liberally and upbraideth not; and it shall be given him" (James 1:5).

Christian growth and maturity do not come unexpectedly to a fortunate few. They are available to all, but precious few are willing to pay their high price. In this chapter, two crucial matters will be studied which relate to our theme of going on to maturity: *self-discipline* and *decision making*. Some specific biblical counsel will be given on these subjects which can help you – if you are willing to put it into practice.

A Christian's Discipline of Self

Self-discipline is a necessary element of Christian discipleship. Returning to Paul's picture of the Christian life as an athletic contest (1 Cor.9:24-27), William Barclay has given a very interesting analysis of this passage. In part, he writes:

> To win this fight and to be victorious in this race demands discipline. We have to discipline our bodies; it is one of the neglected facts of the spiritual life that

very often spiritual depression springs from nothing else than physical unfitness. If a man is going to do his best work in anything he must bring to it a body as fit as he can make it. We neglect our physical health at our peril. We have to discipline our minds; it is one of the tragedies of life that men refuse to think until they are incapable of thinking. We can never solve problems by refusing to see them or by running away from them. We must discipline our souls; we can do so by facing life's sorrows with calm endurance; life's temptations with all the strength that we can bring to them in the strength of God; life's disappointments with courage. There is not a day when life does not bring us opportunities to discipline our souls. [*The Letters to the Corinthians*, (Philadelphia: Westminster Press, 1956), p. 95.]

The Christian must strive for self-mastery as if everything depended on him, knowing all the time that everything ultimately depends on the Lord. And while *asceticism* is a danger on one extreme, the greater present-day danger is the opposite extreme of *decadence*.

Young people in Communist countries are subjected to an intense and demanding life of training and discipline. Our American way of life accents freedom from rigorous demands and emphasizes relaxation and recreation. If Communism one day conquers the Western world, it will not be its ideology but its strong sense of discipline that accomplishes it.

Recent reports of declining Scholastic Aptitude Test scores underline this problem among young people; less homework and more TV have taken away our intellectual discipline. Obesity and general physical weakness point to the same sort of softness among adults; we do not discipline our bodies as we should. Sin is the proof of the absence of spiritual self-discipline among men and women of all ages.

Mastery and accomplishment go to the disciplined person. An athlete preparing for the Olympics follows a strict diet, exercise program, and skill-development program. He knows that the day he relaxes his effort will be the day that some other person will get the competitive edge over him. A musician prepares for a concert with hours and hours of practice; he doesn't just show up and hope to bluff his way through the performance. Someone who is successful in a business or profession pays a price in terms of long hours and hard work; he is more concerned with getting the task at hand accomplished than with getting away for an extra week's vacation.

In my experience as a teacher on the college level, I have had several students to fail courses unnecessarily. Many more have received the grade of C or D when they were capable of making a B or even an A. Their problem was not mental inability. They simply did not know how to apply themselves to difficult tasks. They were unable to sacrifice the tennis courts for the library. They did not know how to manage their time so as to meet reasonable deadlines. I had conferences with many of them and tried to make some practical suggestions which would help cure their ailment. The following suggestions grow out of those experiences – and my own personal struggle to learn the art of self-discipline. I have tried to broaden them so that a person of any age can use them in whatever life situation he or she has at hand.

144

If you are a Christian, these steps will enable you to live an ordered and disciplined life which will reflect glory to God through your daily responsibilities:

Here are *seven steps to a disciplined life:*

(1) Start *now* to bring your life under control. Good resolves about what you will do next week are generally worthless. You have today, and this moment is the best time to begin pulling the loose ends of your life together.

(2) Develop a regular devotional life for *spiritual discipline.* If you have not done so already, commit yourself to a program of daily Bible reading and prayer such as the one recommended in chapters six and seven of this book. If any part of a human life needs and deserves regular development, it is that part which relates him to God most directly.

(3) Discipline your *intellectual life* by applying your mental energies to worthwhile tasks. If you are a student in school or in a company training program, attend every class, be attentive, take notes, read texts, and work hard at mastering the materials at hand. If you are prone to excuse yourself on this point by saying that you are older and that "old folks can't learn anymore," please don't make this terrible mistake. As we grow older, some of us stop using our learning ability; we let TV and other non-challenging pastimes put our brains into neutral. But there is every good reason not to let this happen to you. Read good literature, develop the fine art of conversation, pursue hobbies that challenge you, etc. Be especially conscious about grammar, logical thought, clear speech, and the basic elements of mental discipline.

(4) *Discipline your body* with proper eating habits, exercise, and rest. Over the years, we have spoken out to

protest drinking, smoking, and the improper use of drugs. We have not spoken against the commoner sins of intemperance, pushing our bodies to the point of exhaustion, and failing to keep them in condition. We are temples of the Spirit of God (1 Cor. 6:19-20), and our bodies are to be presented as living sacrifices to the Almighty (Rom. 12:1-2). It is hypocrisy for older Christians to condemn drug abuse among teen-agers while courting heart attacks and other diseases by our failure to discipline our bodies so as to protect our health.

(5) Don't neglect "little things" which will help establish *the habit of self-discipline.* In an earlier chapter of this book, the principle taught in Luke 16:10 has been stressed: faithfulness in life's smaller tasks precedes the chance to accomplish great things. In our present context of emphasis, this passage has renewed relevance. The disciplined person is neat and well-organized; he gets things done by plan and not through haphazard happenstance; he has a sense of goals and priorities. The life pattern of such a person shows itself in everything he or she sets about to accomplish. So do not make the mistake of thinking that you can be careless about most things in your life and competent in the really big matters. It just doesn't work that way. The habits you establish in the little things will carry through into all others.

(6) Learn to be punctual and *respect time.* The disciplined person is habitually prompt in keeping appointments; the undisciplined individual is known for being tardy. The former values his own time and that of others. Over the years, you have observed that some people are always on time for church activities, while others are never on time. The difference in the two groups is not size of

146

family, distance from the building, or traffic patterns. The difference can be summed up in the word ; oqhabit."

(7) *Tackle your hardest job first each day, and complete what you begin.* Most of the experts who have studied time management recommend making "action lists" (i.e., lists of specific things to be done) for each day. A consultant to a past president of Bethlehem Steel offered him this counsel: "Write down the six most important tasks that you have to do tomorrow. Number them by importance. First thing tomorrow morning look at item one and start working on it until you finish it. Then do item two, and so on until quitting time. Don't be concerned if you haven't finished them all. If you can't by this method, you can't by any other. Try this system every working day." The executive is reported to have said later that this was the most profitable advice he ever received.

I have asked several people whose self-discipline was evident the "secret" to their ability to achieve things. Without exception, the equivalent of this procedure for setting daily goals has been the essence of their responses. It is so simple and obvious —yet so very effective.

If you decide to adopt and follow these seven steps, there are a couple of suggestions you need to keep in mind.

First, in order to learn this type of lifestyle, it may be necessary to take some sheets of paper, plot your first several days in half-hour units, and hold yourself to that schedule in slavish fashion. Until you "get the feel" for this new type of disciplined life, it will be hard work to live it. After all, most of us have lived by an opposite pattern for a long time.

Second, do not allow an occasional major diversion

from your schedule to frustrate you. Special situations arise in everyone's life, and flexibility is demanded in these unique circumstances. Don't use trivial things as excuses for failing to hold to your day's action list, but don't blame yourself when major interruptions demand that you re-work some things in your schedule.

Again, the purpose of these suggested steps to a disciplined life is not to produce an ascetic lifestyle. If is to trim the waste off our use of time and to allow us to feel good about making a positive use of each day to the glory of God. The goal is to point us to obedience to this biblical injunction: "Be very careful, then, how you live – not as unwise but as wise, making the most of every opportunity, because the days are evil" (Eph. 5:15-16 NIV).

Godly Decision Making

Christians often ask about the matter of decision making. Will the Lord actually help me with making right choices? Should we pray for his guidance in such things as education, business, and family matters? The Bible answer to these questions is a resounding "Yes!"

God's *general will* for all of us is given in Holy Scripture. It is expected that each of us shall grow in our knowledge of that Word and be conformed to the image of the Son of God. There is no substitute for a knowledge of the Bible. Jesus said, "If ye abide in my word, then are ye truly my disciples; and ye shall know the truth, and the truth shall make you free" (John 8:31-32).

But what of heaven's *particular will* for my life? Granted that the Bible reveals God's will for all men about salvation and right living, how can I know what to do about marriage, education, career, child rearing, and other special situations of my personal life?

Heaven is not cluttered with little road maps for individual human lives. The notion that God has a personal destiny planned for each of us – whom to marry, how many children to have, careers to pursue, etc. – is a feature of some Eastern religions and Calvinistic theology. It is not part of a biblical understanding of God's dealings with human beings. Heaven respects the human will and does not force destinies upon human beings.

The Bible is the general "map" for our lives, and the particular directions of our individual lives are all within the scope of God's will so long as they do not depart from his overall purpose of bringing us to his eternal fellowship in heaven. How can we be sure we are staying on course with the will of God in all of life's particulars?

First, *always act consistently with the general will of God which you have learned from the Bible.* Never excuse yourself for doing something which is forbidden in the Word of God. Always seek to make the decision that will glorify God and allow your life to be an imitation of Jesus' devotion to the Father in heaven.

Second, *seek counsel from people who are in position to give you good advice.* Talk with Christians who are mature in faith and whose judgment you respect from past experiences with them. They will be able to give you insights into certain things that you may have overlooked because of your inexperience.

Third, *use your intellect on the options open to you.* Weigh all the facts you have gained relevant to your decision. List the pluses and minuses you see for each option open to you.

Fourth, *pray for wisdom from God to make the right choice.* Here again is the promise of the Word to Christians: "If any of you lacks wisdom, he should ask God, who gives generously to all without finding fault, and it will be given to him" (James 1:5 NIV).

God does not "guide" us as if we were dumb animals. That is, he does not put bits into our mouths and pull us this way or that by specific dreams, visions, or other personal revelations of his will. He guides us by the exercise of our understanding, by what one writer has dubbed "sanctified common sense." None dares try to enumerate all the instruments of his providence through which the Lord can influence our hearts and deeds. We simply believe his promises to give us wisdom and to work all things together for good in the lives of people who love him and submit to his Word.

Because we are God's people and have these promises, we must not try to take matters into our own hands with regard to making choices and committing ourselves to far-reaching decisions. Even in the routine and apparently trivial decisions of our lives, we must submit them to him in prayer and seek his guidance.

Conclusion

Christian living is not a church-building phenomenon. It is not a matter of occasional significance. It is a day-by-day and event-by-event exercise. Every aspect of the consecrated disciple's life is touched directly by his enthronement of Jesus Christ as his Sovereign Lord.

It must be our goal to bring every thought and deed into captivity to the obedience of Christ (2 Cor. 10:5). This goal necessitates the daily discipline of ourselves and godly decision making. Without them, we are doomed to perpetual immaturity in spiritual matters and can never go on to maturity in Christ.

Some Things To Think About

1. Is the matter of self-discipline important to you? What about decision making? What general guidelines have you followed up to this point in life which have been helpful to you in these areas?

2. Self-discipline is a habit which carries over into every area of one's life. Can one who is careless and sloppy about his or her appearance, work, or personal habits be self-disciplined in spiritual matters?

3. What is your reaction to Dr. Barclay's analysis of 1 Corinthians 9:24-27? What would you add to it?

4. Review each of the "seven steps to a disciplined life" given in this chapter. Analyze your own habits in light of them. Do you think these steps are practical and sound?

5. What is the difference between *asceticism* and *decadence*? Must one choose between these two alternatives? Describe a Christian lifestyle as a third alternative to them.

6. What is God's *general will?* How can we know his *particular will* for our lives? How does God guide the lives of men and women today?

7. What suggestion(s) from this chapter do you find most helpful to your own life situation? Can you benefit from it/them in your daily life?

Chapter Twelve

PASS IT ON!

Here is the ultimate test of one's spirituality: *Can I get across to other people the saving truth of the gospel?* If not, what good are you to a lost world? If not, of what value are you to Jesus Christ?

Soul-winning is at the very heart of the process of going on to maturity in the Christian life.

Liberal theology has redefined evangelism so as to equate it with social reform, but Scripture defines it as preaching Jesus Christ. An "evangelist" (Gr, *euangelistes*) is a messenger with good news, a preacher of the gospel. Our English word "evangelism" is defined as the winning or revival of personal commitments to Christ. If you are not making a contribution to this work, you are not fulfilling your primary role as a Christian.

CHRIST'S COMMAND: GO AND TEACH

Christianity is a religion of redeeming actions. "God so *loved* the world ... " (John 3:16). Jesus "*gave himself* for your sins ... " (Gal. 1:4). The Holy Spirit came upon the apostles to "*teach* you all things ... " (John 14:26). The saved are those who "*do the will* of the Father ... " (Matt. 7:21).

As Jesus was about to return to his glory with the Father and Holy Spirit in heaven, he gave this final commission to his apostles: "And he said unto them, Go ye into all the world, and preach the gospel to the whole creation" (Mark 16:15). These men were faithful to their task, and many of them gave up their very lives in order to tell the story of redeeming grace. As a result of their preaching, the church of Christ was established throughout the Roman Empire of the first century.

The movement thus begun was not to end with their ministries, however. It was destined to be perpetuated until the time of Jesus' second coming. Thus the apostles commissioned others to preach the Word of God, and told them to commission others, etc. For example, Paul wrote one of his preaching assistants these words: "And the things which thou hast heard from me among many witnesses, the same commit thou to faithful men, who shall be able to teach others also" (2 Tim. 2:2). This process is still repeating itself in our generation.

Christians have been saved "that we might bring forth fruit unto God" (Rom. 7:4), and God expects each of us to bear fruit. There can be no fruitfulness apart from dependence on Jesus, who is our life (cf. John 15:1ff). Neither does every plant in the divine vineyard bear the same type of fruit or at the same rate. But each one is supposed to bear fruit.

Using this analogy of the church as the vineyard of God, Paul made some very important points in writing to the saints at Corinth. "What then is Apollos? and what is Paul? Ministers through whom ye believed; and each as the Lord gave to him. I planted, Apollos watered; but God gave the increase. So then neither is he that planteth anything, neither he that watereth; but God that giveth the increase. Now he that planteth and he that watereth are one: but each shall receive his own reward according to his own labor" (1 Cor. 3:5-8).

First, notice that *different people have different roles in soul-winning*. Some plant, others water, etc. Some people are public teachers of the gospel, and others bring their neighbors who can be taught. Some go to the mission field, and others support their work. Some open their homes as centers for private teaching of the Word of God, and others are learners and encouragers of this ministry. Not every Christian does the same thing in our ministry of the gospel, but each makes some contribution to the total effort.

Second, *it is God who gives the increase.* Let us never get so caught up in a man or a method that we forget where the power to save sinners comes from. The gospel is God's power to save (Rom. 1:16), and the praise for any individual's salvation goes to him.

Third, each Christian who participates in the process of getting the gospel to a lost person will be *rewarded* "according to his own labor."

Before soul-winning can be a *program,* it must first be

a *passion* in our hearts. We must love God and the lost enough to become involved in the process of evangelism.

The story is told of a brother who led the closing prayer at the last service of a gospel meeting and said, "Lord, if any spark of revival has been lit in this meeting, we pray that you will water the spark." If the story is true, one hopes that the man simply mixed his metaphors! Yet as the lethargy of some Christians and congregations is witnessed, one does have occasion to wonder who "watered the spark" of evangelism among us.

Perhaps we need to re-think the very foundation principles of the work of evangelism.

Presuppositions of Soul-Winning

There are three essential convictions which underlie soul-winning. Take away any one – much less all three – of them, and there will be no evangelism. As we look at each of them, make the following question a personal one: Do I believe this?

Men and women not in Christ are lost.

Sin is the worst thing in human experience, for it separates men and women from God. "Your iniquities have separated between you and your God, and your sins have hid his face from you, so that he will not hear" (Isa. 59:2). When the Lord comes in Judgment, he will be "rendering vengeance to them that know not God, and to them that obey not the gospel of our Lord Jesus" (2 Thess. 1:8). This means that a great many people we know are headed for eternal ruin – unless we get the message of redemption to them. Yet people can get more upset over lost care keys or credit cards than lost souls.

As I am writing this, a lady who lives less than one

block from my office is frantic over her lost dachshund. She has searched the neighborhood, published a notice of a reward for its return, and is leaving no stone unturned in her efforts to find it. I do not begrudge her efforts and hope she finds her pet. But how many lost souls are the objects of so much concern?

The gospel is God's power to save the lost.

"For I am not ashamed of the gospel: for it is the power of God unto salvation to every one that believeth" (Rom. 1:16).

If a Christian really believes that the gospel has divine power inherent in it, he will not be reluctant to share it with someone. In fact, he will be able to tell the story expectantly. He knows that its effect depends not on his ability as a presenter but on the power of the message itself. We must never come to the point of too great a reliance on techniques and gimmicks. We must believe that the power is of God and that it is felt every time the gospel is taught.

Something will happen in the act of sharing the gospel.

Given the power of the gospel and a human to hear it taught, there will be a reaction. The gospel is of such a nature that the person who hears it cannot remain unaffected. The heart of Lydia was "opened" when she heard the story of Christ (Acts 16:14), and the people who heard Peter on Pentecost were "pricked in their hearts" by what they heard (Acts 2:37). At the same time, we must be prepared for negative reactions as well. Some people "mock" the gospel in their unbelief and turn away from it with powerful antagonism (cf. Acts 17:32-34).

The Word of God is not a cherished heirloom to be set on a shelf, prized, and scrutinized. It is a seed to be planted, a fire to be lit, a bomb to be exploded. Whatever image you choose to use, fix the concept in your mind that the gospel is power at your disposal – power which you can unleash by telling the story of Christ.

If you don't believe that people without it are lost, you will be unconcerned about evangelism. Your view will be that people are fine just as they are and don't need the news about Jesus. If you don't believe that the gospel is God's power to save, you will have no motivation to share it. The Bible will be nothing more than just a book which some people read and some do not. If you don't believe that something will happen in the act of teaching the Word of God, you will be careless about your opportunities to share its truth with individuals who do not know it. Evangelism will be merely a word and preaching the gospel merely a task to be completed.

For the purpose of this study, let us assume that you believe these presuppositions of soul-winning and want to be involved directly in the work of evangelism. The next step is to have a workable method to use in sharing the gospel.

How to Go About the Task

Know the Word of God. Since the power to convert lost souls is in the gospel message itself, you must know it thoroughly and learn to rely on its power. This underscores the need of your daily study of the Bible which was discussed in Chapter Six. The Word of God is a powerful weapon, but it functions most effectively only when it is handled by trained hands. Especially should you know and have memorized the passages which relate directly to the plan of salvation. You will find that every fact you learn from your study of Scripture will be useful to you at one time or another in your teaching efforts.

As to some specific passages which can be used in teaching the will of God for a sinner's redemption, here are some you will find useful: on the nature of the gospel message and its fundamental facts – 1 Corinthians 15:1-4 and Ephesians 2:1-10; on the necessity of faith -Hebrews 11:6 and John 8:24; on the necessity of repentance – Luke 13:3 and Acts 17:30-31; on the necessity of public confession of one's faith in Christ -Matthew 10:32 and Romans 10:10; on the necessity of baptism – Acts 2:38 and Romans 6:4. If you are making an appeal to an erring Christian, you should be familiar with passages such as Acts 8:22 and James 5:16.

Know How to Share the Message. You need to have a basic approach in mind as to how to present the facts of the gospel to a person. I certainly do not oppose the use of visual aids and other effective teaching devices in presenting the Word of God to people. But a soul-winning Christian should be ready in any situation for the opportunity to present Christ. This means that you need a simple and uncomplicated means by which you can teach people how to be saved.

Here is an effective three-step outline which could be used in most any situation in presenting the message of Christ: (1) All men are sinners and lost, (2) Christ is the only one who can save, and (3) Jesus saves only those who will obey him.

These three points – made in this order – can be worked into almost any conversation about spiritual topics. It is usable on an airplane, talking with someone at his door, when someone comes to you for counsel, etc. It is adaptable to non-Christians or wayward saints. It can be used at whatever level of knowledge the individual has about the Word of God.

Imagine that someone has started talking with you about some problem in his or her life. This is a common event, and it affords a perfect opportunity to use the approach for presenting the gospel as outlined above. After the person has talked a while about the situation, you can respond by saying, "Sue, the thing that causes all our problems is sin. I am a Christian, and I believe what the Bible teaches about how our transgressions of the will of God separate us from him and spoil the happiness that he wants us to have in this life." This is usually all the opening you will need to turn the conversation to the Bible. You might look at passages such as Romans 3:23 and 6:23 with her at this point.

Then it is a natural second step to say, "And the only one who can help us with this sin problem is Jesus Christ." Read a verse like Acts 4:12, and talk about the meaning of the life and death of the Son of Man. If will not be long, in most cases, until you will find an appropriate place to say, "Sue, Jesus has promised to save everyone who will obey the Word of God. That means that he is able and willing to save you." Here you will want to look at verses like Matthew 7:21 or Hebrews 5:9 and proceed to lay out the plan of salvation in a clear and deliberate manner.

This is a very simple approach and requires no paraphernalia, special setting, or detailed training. It outlines the individual's basic responsibility for his or her salvation. If no decision is made at that time, you have established a background of discussing the Word of God with the person that can be built on later.

Pray. Always be prayerful about lost souls. Pray daily for opportunities to tell others about Christ. Most of us have more chances to speak about Christ than we use. But if it seems to you that you receive very few, could it be that "you have not because you ask not"? (Jas. 4:2b). Then be prayerful for particular individuals that you have the opportunity to teach. Ask the Lord to help you be wise in your attempts at teaching them. Ask him to bring circumstances to bear in their lives which will make them responsive and sensitive to the Word.

Be Loving. It is necessary to use godly tact and boldness in proper combination. Nothing is so sure to turn people away as a "professional evangelist" who is artificial and brassy in his approach. Yet one cannot use fear of that image as an excuse for refusing to be involved in the work of winning souls to Christ. The best solution to avoiding these extremes is to be natural, warm, and caring in your approach.

Take the example of Jesus in talking with the Samaritan woman by Jacob's well as your model (John 4:1-42). He began his conversation with her by talking about the water she had come to draw from the well. Just as people need water to sustain their physical lives, he continued, so do they also need "living water" for the sake of their eternal welfare (v. 10).

As they discussed what Jesus meant by saying this, he guided her into deeper thinking about God and her relationship with him. When they came to the touchy matter of her manner of life, the Lord gently but firmly rebuked

161

her sinfulness in that she was living with a man to whom she had no moral right (v.18). He was tactful, yet bold; he considered her feelings, but his first concern was to speak the full truth she needed to hear.

Be Sincere. Let the people with whom you speak know that you are genuinely concerned about them, that you love them, that you want them to be saved.

Live Your Commitment. Keep your life pure lest you become a stumbling block to the people you attempt to teach. They have a right to expect you to take seriously and live by the high moral expectations of the gospel you are trying to get them to believe and obey.

Conclusion

In the preface to his translation of the book of Acts (*The Young Church in Action*), J. B. Phillips wrote:

> In the pages of this unpretentious book, written by the author of the third Gospel, the fresh air of heaven is plainly blowing. Many problems comparable to modern complexities never arise here because the men and women concerned were of one heart and mind in the Spirit. Many another issue is never allowed to arise because these early Christians were led by the Spirit to the main task of bringing people to God through Christ and were not permitted to enjoy fascinating sidetracts.

What "fascinating sidetracks" are we pursuing which keep us from the true work of God in this world? Won't you resolve to become directly involved in the work of soul-winning? It is crucial in your own spiritual life in moving you toward greater maturity. It is crucial in the lives of those people that you have it in your power to reach.

Some Things To Think About

1. What is evangelism? Whose responsibility is it? Who should be involved in doing this spiritual work?

2. Study Paul's analogy of the church as the vineyard of God. What are some of the primary lessons to be gained from it?

3. Review each of the presuppositions of soul-winning given in this chapter. How many of the three do you believe?

4. Suppose someone asked you this question: "What must I do to be saved?" Could you answer the question with appropriate Bible passages?

5. A three-point plan for presenting the gospel is suggested in this chapter. Analyze it. How practical is it? Can it be helpful to you?

6. Whom do you consider to be the most likely person among your acquaintances for conversion? What can you do to initiate the process of leading him or her to Christ?

7. A quotation from J. B. Phillips speaks of "fascinating sidetracks." What does he mean by that term? Is it possible that we have chosen some of them over the primary business of God in our world?

APPENDIX A

Luke 7:1-10 (Jesus Heals a Centurion's Servant).

Capernaum—NW shore of Sea of Galilee; Jesus lived here for a while, and several events of his ministry center here; a synagoge has been excavated which is likely on the same site as the one in this story.

Centurion—commander of 100 Roman soldiers *thus a Gentile.

Same incident related in Matt. 8:5-13 where a statement is given of God's intention to give Gentiles like this man a chance to enter the Kingdom.

Summary: In response to the humble faith of a Roman centurion, Jesus healed the man's servant and observed how much more faith this Gentile had than most Jews.

Note: This makes me think of Cornelius.

Memorize verse 9.

Pray for the kind of faith this man showed.